Selected Topics in Child and Adolescent Mental Health

*Edited by Samuel Stones,
Jonathan Glazzard and Maria Rosaria Muzio*

Published in London, United Kingdom

IntechOpen

Supporting open minds since 2005

Selected Topics in Child and Adolescent Mental Health
http://dx.doi.org/10.5772/intechopen.77757
Edited by Samuel Stones, Jonathan Glazzard and Maria Rosaria Muzio

Contributors
Jonathan Glazzard, Samuel Oliver James Stones, Florence Levy, Martha Escobar Lux, Perrine Heymann, Daniel Bagner, Brynna Heflin, Cringu Antoniu Ionescu, Alexandra Matei, Juan Manuel Escobar, Minshull Maryjane, Galloway-Walker Stuart

© The Editor(s) and the Author(s) 2020
The rights of the editor(s) and the author(s) have been asserted in accordance with the Copyright, Designs and Patents Act 1988. All rights to the book as a whole are reserved by INTECHOPEN LIMITED. The book as a whole (compilation) cannot be reproduced, distributed or used for commercial or non-commercial purposes without INTECHOPEN LIMITED's written permission. Enquiries concerning the use of the book should be directed to INTECHOPEN LIMITED rights and permissions department (permissions@intechopen.com).
Violations are liable to prosecution under the governing Copyright Law.

(cc) BY

Individual chapters of this publication are distributed under the terms of the Creative Commons Attribution 3.0 Unported License which permits commercial use, distribution and reproduction of the individual chapters, provided the original author(s) and source publication are appropriately acknowledged. If so indicated, certain images may not be included under the Creative Commons license. In such cases users will need to obtain permission from the license holder to reproduce the material. More details and guidelines concerning content reuse and adaptation can be found at http://www.intechopen.com/copyright-policy.html.

Notice
Statements and opinions expressed in the chapters are these of the individual contributors and not necessarily those of the editors or publisher. No responsibility is accepted for the accuracy of information contained in the published chapters. The publisher assumes no responsibility for any damage or injury to persons or property arising out of the use of any materials, instructions, methods or ideas contained in the book.

First published in London, United Kingdom, 2020 by IntechOpen
IntechOpen is the global imprint of INTECHOPEN LIMITED, registered in England and Wales, registration number: 11086078, 7th floor, 10 Lower Thames Street, London, EC3R 6AF, United Kingdom
Printed in Croatia

British Library Cataloguing-in-Publication Data
A catalogue record for this book is available from the British Library

Additional hard and PDF copies can be obtained from orders@intechopen.com

Selected Topics in Child and Adolescent Mental Health
Edited by Samuel Stones, Jonathan Glazzard and Maria Rosaria Muzio
p. cm.
Print ISBN 978-1-78985-269-1
Online ISBN 978-1-78985-270-7
eBook (PDF) ISBN 978-1-83880-364-3

We are IntechOpen,
the world's leading publisher of Open Access books
Built by scientists, for scientists

4,900+
Open access books available

123,000+
International authors and editors

140M+
Downloads

151
Countries delivered to

Our authors are among the
Top 1%
most cited scientists

12.2%
Contributors from top 500 universities

WEB OF SCIENCE™

Selection of our books indexed in the Book Citation Index
in Web of Science™ Core Collection (BKCI)

Interested in publishing with us?
Contact book.department@intechopen.com

Numbers displayed above are based on latest data collected.
For more information visit www.intechopen.com

Meet the editors

Professor Jonathan Glazzard is a Professor of Inclusive Education in the Carnegie School of Education. His research focuses on a broad range of topics and disciplines, including mental health, LGBTQ+ inclusion, special educational needs, critical disability studies, critical psychology, sociology and early literacy development. Jonathan uses a broad range of approaches, including narrative methodology, visual/participatory methodologies and more traditional interviews and focus groups. Prof. Glazzard's recent projects include exploration of headteacher resilience, teacher mental health and the experiences of teachers who identify as LGBTQ+. He is deeply committed to research that advances inclusion and social justice for marginalised groups and individuals. Prof. Glazzard is a Course Leader and Director of Studies and supervisor for several MRes, EdD and PhD students.

Samuel Stones is a lecturer and doctoral researcher in the Carnegie School of Education at Leeds Beckett University. His research outputs are linked with the Centre for LGBTQ+ Inclusion in Education and the Carnegie Centre of Excellence for Mental Health in Schools. His research explores the experiences of teachers who identify as Lesbian, Gay, Bisexual and Trans, with emphasis on the impact of sexual orientation on resilience, agency and identity. Mr. Stones supervises students on a range of postgraduate courses and he works with initial teacher training students in university and school contexts. He also holds a national training role for a Multi-Academy Trust and is an Associate Leader and Head of Year at a secondary school and sixth form college.

Maria Rosaria Muzio, MD, works at the Division of Infantile Neuropsychiatry, UOMI - Maternal and Infant Health, Asl Na 3 Sud, Torre del Greco, Naples, where she is responsible for Infantile Neuropsychiatry. Dr Muzio graduated in Medicine and Surgery with honours in 1997 at the University 'Vanvitelli' of Naples and then undertook postgraduate studies in Child Neuropsychiatry, magna cum laude, gaining her doctorate in 2002. Dr. Muzio acts as editorial board member for several medical journals. She has been a speaker at numerous conferences and conventions, and is the author of scientific publications, book chapters, etc. in the fields of child neuropsychiatry, cognitive impairment, pain assessment in developmental disorders, autism spectrum disorders, genetic disorders, neuropsychological features of anesthesia and nutraceutical research.

Contents

Preface — XI

Chapter 1 — 1
Introductory Chapter: Selected Topics in Child and Adolescent Mental Health
by Jonathan Glazzard and Samuel Stones

Chapter 2 — 7
Social Media and Young People's Mental Health
by Jonathan Glazzard and Samuel Stones

Chapter 3 — 21
Parent-Child Interaction Therapy: Theory and Research to Practice
by Perrine Heymann, Brynna H. Heflin and Daniel M. Bagner

Chapter 4 — 35
Where Technology Meets Psychology: Improving Global Mental Health
by Martha Escobar Lux and Juan Manuel Escobar

Chapter 5 — 47
Pregnancy in Adolescence: A Hallmark of Forthcoming Perinatal Depression?
by Alexandra Matei and Cringu Antoniu Ionescu

Chapter 6 — 61
Working Memory, Language, Reading and Behavior: The Importance of Laterality, Symbolism and Default Networks
by Levy Florence, Minshull Maryjane and Galloway-Walker Stuart

Preface

This book focuses on a variety of critical themes that relate to child and adolescent mental health and working memory. It addresses various theoretical perspectives as well as highlighting implications for practice. The topics addressed include social media and mental health, parent-child interaction therapy (PCIT), the role of e-learning in mental health, perinatal depression and working memory, language, reading and behaviour. In focusing on mental ill-health, this book addresses a global concern. The causes of poor mental health are complex and multi-faceted. In acknowledging this complexity, it must be recognized that there is no single 'magic bullet' that will solve the problem. A multidisciplinary approach is therefore required to address the issues, including a variety of interventions. In addition, the book emphasizes the important contributions that schools, health and social care services and families can provide about addressing the mental health challenges experienced by children and young people.

Chapter 1 is the Introductory chapter that outlines the content of this book. It provides a brief overview of the content of each chapter and summarises the key points made by the authors.

Chapter 2 addresses the role of social media in child and adolescent mental health. Glazzard and Stones highlight the detrimental impact of social media use on young people's mental health through exploring themes such as bullying, body-esteem, sleep deprivation and self-harm. Moreover, they highlight the potential benefits of social media use on young people's mental health and they draw on empirical data from young people to substantiate their arguments. The authors emphasize that schools play a crucial role in developing young people's skills in digital literacy and digital resilience and they highlight the importance of fostering young people's understanding of digital citizenship through the digital curriculum. However, the authors also stress that schools are not solely responsible for addressing the issues that are raised in the chapter. Advertising and social media companies play a crucial role in keeping children safe and parents also have a responsibility not only in limiting children's exposure to screen time but also in educating their children about safe and responsible use of social media.

Chapter 3 explores the role of parent-child interaction therapy (PCIT) in supporting children's behaviour. Heymann, Heflin and Bagner present a clear rationale for this intervention that involves the use of a wireless headset to coach parents or carers during the process of interaction with the child. The strategy is underpinned both by attachment theory and social learning theory and stems from the principles of play therapy. The authors review research that has examined PCIT with a variety of diverse population settings and formats. They present a case study of PCIT with a child younger than 2 years to demonstrate the effectiveness of PCIT and highlight some common challenges and pitfalls that clinicians may face in clinical practice. They argue that the strategy enhances parent-child/adult-child relationships and through a case study they demonstrate that the intervention was successful in reducing aggression, non-compliant behaviour and parental stress.

In Chapter 4, Lux and Escobar discuss the role of e-learning for health care providers, including the role of e-learning to support professional development in mental health for health care professionals. The authors highlight some significant challenges for health care providers. One in four people worldwide will suffer from depression, anxiety, or some other form of mental illness over their lifetime. Health care providers experience heavy caseloads and therefore have limited time to meet the increasing demand for services for mental health support. E-learning allows individuals to study at their own pace, it is financially viable and sufficiently flexible. The authors argue that e-mental health learning has the potential to be used for health care promotion, prevention, early intervention and treatment. E-mental health learning, indeed, can compensate for the shortage of health care providers and it can provide interactive learning opportunities. Lux and Escobar outline some of the barriers that may be associated with e-mental health learning but they present a convincing argument for adopting this approach.

In Chapter 5, Matei and Ionescu outline the issues of perinatal depression. The chapter highlights that the risk of depression in teenagers both during and after pregnancy is higher than for adults. The chapter emphasizes the need for parental and peer support and the importance of meeting the holistic needs of the individual. The chapter reviews a range of interventions to support perinatal depression including the use of medication, complementary medicine and psychotherapy. The chapter emphasizes the need for a multidisciplinary approach to support adolescents who experience perinatal depression. Matei and Ionescu argue that perinatal depression is a serious concern which, if left untreated, exposes the mother and child to risks.

In Chapter 6, Florence, Maryjane and Stuart explore the importance of working memory for cognitive development and language-related reading skills. This chapter is extensively theoretically underpinned and makes an important contribution to knowledge. The authors argue that the capacity for symbolic representation in the working memory is likely to be important to orthographic and comprehension skills. The authors conclude that 'the interaction of language, early reading and attentional skills has important implications for future studies of kindergarten readiness and gender differences in preschool children'.

We thank all contributors to this book for their well-researched and engaging chapters. Each chapter has highlighted pertinent issues that relate to the topic and implications for practice have been identified.

Samuel Stones and Jonathan Glazzard
Carnegie School of Education,
Leeds Beckett University,
Leeds England

Maria Rosaria Muzio
Division of Infantile Neuropsychiatry,
UOMI - Maternal and Infant Health,
Torre del Greco, Naples, Italy

Chapter 1

Introductory Chapter: Selected Topics in Child and Adolescent Mental Health

Jonathan Glazzard and Samuel Stones

1. Child and adolescent mental health: context, causes and solutions

Improving people's mental health has been identified as one of the most critical public health priorities [1, 2]. Child and adolescent mental health is a global concern, and although each nation faces its own unique challenges, there are common concerns, challenges and solutions to this problem. Statistics suggest that mental ill health in children and young people is increasing. Research suggests that half of all psychological disorders begin before the age of 14 years [3]. However, the increase in diagnoses may also be attributed to the de-stigmatisation of mental ill health in recent years, increasing awareness of mental health among professionals and government investment in mental health research. It is important to remember that stigmatising and deficit discourses associated with mental ill health over the last century resulted in its concealment and internalised shame.

2. Whole school approach

Recent efforts by nations to eradicate the stigma associated with mental health have resulted in increased awareness of mental health among children, young people, professionals and parents. In some countries (e.g. the United Kingdom), it is statutory to provide children and adolescents with a mental health curriculum. Research demonstrates that educating young people about mental health not only increases their mental health literacy, it has a positive effect on their attitudes towards mental health and increases help-seeking behaviours [4]. However, providing young people with a mental health curriculum is only one part of a whole school or college approach to mental health. Educational institutions which have positive cultures promote a sense of belonging which is critical for positive mental health. In addition, schools and colleges need to consider approaches for working in partnership with young people, parents and health and social care professionals to ensure that young people's holistic needs are met. Approaches to identification of mental ill health need to be proactive rather than reactive. Often, mental ill health is identified through observing changes in a child's mood, behaviour or physical appearance. The problem with this type of reactive approach is that it fails to identify those young people who do not demonstrate these obvious signs. A proactive approach which incorporates universal screening ensures that children who do not demonstrate visible signs of mental ill health, but actually experience it, can be identified.

3. A clinical model

Within some countries, in recent years there has been a focus on providing in-school interventions to support children and young people's mental health. These vary from universal interventions which are available to all children (e.g. a mental health curriculum), to group and highly personalised individual interventions. In the United Kingdom, there has been government investment into training a new group of professionals—education and mental health practitioners. These professionals are deployed to work in schools alongside teachers. Their role is to provide low-level clinical interventions, including counselling, cognitive behaviour therapy and other therapies, so that young people can receive mental health support within their school contexts. Although it might be argued that this is a positive step in the right direction, it also reflects a clinical model which fails to address the root causes of mental ill health.

4. Finding solutions by addressing the causes

The solutions of mental ill health in childhood need to be found by identifying the causes of it. If the root causes are not addressed, then societies risk only addressing mental ill health at a surface level. The causes of mental ill health in childhood and adolescence are complex and multifaceted. The biopsychosocial model of health [5] demonstrates how mental health is a product of overlapping biological, social and psychological factors. In some cases, poor mental health is rooted in the individual. Those with disabilities are more likely to experience mental ill health. Young people with autistic spectrum conditions are likely to experience stress due to sensory sensitivities which are linked with their autism. However, often the causes of poor mental health are rooted in social circumstances. Young people living in social deprived communities are more likely to experience poor mental health. According to the Mental Health Foundation [6]:

> *A growing body of evidence, mainly from high-income countries, has shown that there is a strong socioeconomic gradient in mental health, with people of lower socioeconomic status having a higher likelihood of developing and experiencing mental health problems. In other words, social inequalities in society are strongly linked to mental health inequalities.*

Children who experience parental conflict, neglect, abuse and poor parental mental health are at a heightened risk of developing mental ill health [7]. Children who form weak attachments with their primary caregiver are also at increased risk of developing mental ill health. We also know that school-related factors play a role in mental ill health. Limited curriculum choice and examination stress are also factors which result in poor mental health [8]. In addition, exposure to bullying in school can result in young people not feeling safe and therefore not experiencing a sense of belonging.

Meyer's model of minority stress [9] is a useful conceptual framework which demonstrates that individuals with a minority status are more likely to experience poor mental health. The model identifies three stressors which include general stressors and distal and proximal stressors. According to the model, general stressors may include financial-, employment-, relationship- or housing-related stressors which most people experience. However, individuals with a minority status may experience additional stressors which result in poor mental health. Distal stressors relate to exposure to bullying, prejudice and discrimination as a result of their minority status, whilst proximal stress is the internalised stress that results from the anticipation that individuals with a minority status will encounter distal stressors. The model demonstrates how race, sexuality, gender and disability can result in poor mental health as a result of exposure or anticipation of exposure to prejudice, discrimination and bullying.

5. Responding at a systemic level

As we have demonstrated above, the causes of mental ill health in childhood and adolescence are often rooted in social circumstances. Therefore, it could be argued that intervention at the level of the individual is insufficient. A clinical model which focuses on therapeutic intervention will address the symptoms of mental ill health, but it will not address the factors which have caused it to occur in the first place. Children and adolescents who receive therapy still have to continue to live their lives in homes, communities and schools which are often the cause of poor mental health. Governments therefore need to adopt a response which addresses the systemic factors which cause poor mental health. These factors include poverty, adverse childhood experiences, societal prejudice and discrimination (including racism, sexism, ageism, homophobia, biphobia and transphobia and disablism) and the structures which underpin the education system.

Adolescents who are not in education, employment or training also risk developing poor mental health. Therefore, investment in this area is vital to secure positive outcomes for young people. Providing young people with a relevant curriculum which meets their needs and prepares them for employment will ensure that they have the knowledge, skills, motivation and qualifications to secure employment. Providing curriculum breadth and balance and broadening out what constitutes academic achievement will support young people to stay motivated and engaged in their learning as well as supporting aspiration. This needs to be matched by government investment in education, employment and training to ensure that opportunities are available to all young people, irrespective of their social backgrounds.

Although a clinical model can promote resilience, resilience is not just rooted within individuals. Resilience is dynamic and changes in different contexts. Although individual factors play a role in supporting resilience (e.g. sense of hope, sense of purpose, self-worth and self-efficacy), resilience is supported through access to social networks and relationships [10]. Positive relationships with peers, family members and teachers help to support resilience. Resilience is influenced by family, community and school contexts, the nature of the challenges that individuals are exposed to and the broader policy and legislative framework which influences the lives of individuals [10]. Resilience interventions in education locate resilience within the individual rather than acknowledging that the individual is not solely responsible for their own resilience.

The relationship between technology and mental ill health has been identified in several studies [11, 12]. Schools play an important role in developing young people's digital literacy and awareness of digital citizenship so that they can be responsible users of technology. Schools also play a crucial role in supporting young people to critically engage with digital content so that they can evaluate it. However, despite the risks associated with technology and social media specifically, the benefits outweigh the limitations. Technology enables young people to network, access support and advice and to function as global, connected citizens, all of which are vital for good mental health.

It is clear that improving people's mental health is a priority [1, 2]. Destigmatising mental ill health is crucial in order to support effective diagnoses, and it is essential that action is taken to continue raising awareness of mental health among professionals but also at a governmental level. Education will continue to play a vital role in relation to mental health literacy and attitudes towards mental health [4], and the whole school or college approach is essential to promote a sense of belonging. However, educational institutions must also be proactive in establishing and developing partnerships with stakeholders to ensure that young people's needs are met holistically. These approaches and mechanisms for promoting positive mental health must acknowledge the heightened risk of poor mental health for those with experiences of conflict, neglect and abuse as well as those with a minority status [9].

Likewise, adolescents who are not in education, employment or training are also at a heightened risk of developing poor mental health. For these young people, government investment plays a critical role in providing opportunities to all, irrespective of social background. Young people must be equipped with the knowledge, skills, motivation and qualifications required to secure employment, and educational institutions cannot meet these needs unless they are prioritised at a governmental level. Social networks, relationships and the educational curriculum are essential to positive mental health, and these must be supported holistically by broader policy and legislative frameworks within and throughout society [10].

Author details

Jonathan Glazzard* and Samuel Stones
Leeds Beckett University, Leeds, UK

*Address all correspondence to: j.glazzard@leedsbeckett.ac.uk

IntechOpen

© 2020 The Author(s). Licensee IntechOpen. This chapter is distributed under the terms of the Creative Commons Attribution License (http://creativecommons.org/licenses/by/3.0), which permits unrestricted use, distribution, and reproduction in any medium, provided the original work is properly cited.

References

[1] Kieling C, Baker-Henningham H, Belfer M, Conti G, Ertem I, Omigbodun O, et al. Child and adolescent mental health worldwide: Evidence for action. The Lancet. 2011;**378**:1515-1525

[2] Knifton L, Quinn N. Public Mental Health: Global Perspectives. Berkshire, UK: McGraw-Hill; 2013

[3] Kessler RC, Angermeyer M, Anthony JC, De Graaf R, Demyttenaere K, Gasquet I, et al. Lifetime prevalence and age-of-onset distributions of mental disorders in the World Health Organization's world mental health survey initiative. World Psychiatry. 2007;**6**(3):168-176

[4] Corrigan P, Watson A. How children stigmatize people with mental illness. The International Journal of Social Psychiatry. 2007;**53**:526-546

[5] World Health Organisation. Towards a Common Language for Functioning, Disability and Health. The International Classification of Functioning, Disability and Health. Geneva: World Health Organisation; 2001

[6] Mental Health Foundation (MHF). Fundamental Facts about Mental Health 2016. London: Mental Health Foundation; 2016

[7] Crenna-Jennings W, Hutchinson J. Access to Children and Young People's Mental Health Services—2018. London: Education Policy Institute; 2018

[8] House of Commons. The Government's Green Paper on Mental Health: Failing a Generation. House of Commons Education and Health and Social Care Committees. 2018

[9] Meyer IH. Prejudice, social stress, and mental health in lesbian, gay and bisexual populations: Conceptual issues and research evidence. Psychological Bulletin. 2003;**129**(5):674-697

[10] Roffey S. Ordinary magic needs ordinary magicians: The power and practice of positive relationships for building youth resilience and wellbeing. Kognition and Paedagogik. 2017;**103**:38-57. Available from: https://dpf.dk/produktkategori/kognition-paedagogik

[11] Frith E. Social Media and Children's Mental Health: A Review of the Evidence. London: Education Policy Institute; 2017

[12] Royal Society for Public Health (RSPH). #StatusOfMind: Social Media and Young People's Mental Health and Wellbeing. London: Royal Society for Public Health; 2017

Chapter 2

Social Media and Young People's Mental Health

Jonathan Glazzard and Samuel Stones

Abstract

Evidence suggests that social media can impact detrimentally on children and young people's mental health. At the same time, social media use can be beneficial and have positive effects. This chapter outlines the detrimental and positive effects of social media use for young people. Schools play a critical role in educating young people about how to use social media safely and responsibly. However, schools cannot address all the issues and parents, social media and advertising companies also have a responsibility to protect children and young people from harm. This chapter outlines some of the potential solutions to the issues that are identified.

Keywords: social media, mental health, technology, children, young people

1. Introduction

In England Anne Longfield, England's Children's Commissioner, has written to the biggest social media companies, urging them to commit to tackling issues of disturbing content. Her letter follows the suicide of 14-year-old Molly Russell, who tragically killed herself after viewing distressing self-harm images on Instagram. The letter urges social media companies to back the introduction of a statutory duty of care where they would have to prioritise the safety and wellbeing of children using their platforms. Ms. Longfield's letter ends with the following message to the digital industry:

> *With great power comes great responsibility and it is your responsibility to support measures that give children the information and tools they need growing up in this digital world—or to admit that you cannot control what anyone sees on your platforms.*

According to literature use of the internet has risen rapidly in the last decade [1]. The way in which young people interact has changed significantly over the last decade. Social media enables them to develop online connections with people within their immediate friendship group but also to form connects with people who are more geographically dispersed. As a result of the digital revolution in recent years, young people are now able to communicate with others more efficiently and gain access to knowledge and advice more rapidly. For those living in rural communities, social media can facilitate social communications which otherwise would not be possible.

My own discussions with young people in schools indicates that social media is an extremely important part of their daily lives. It brings many benefits but is also exposes them to risks. Young people are often very aware of these risks and understand how to keep themselves safe. However, sadly this does not prevent all of them from harm, as is evident through recent cases of teenage suicides as a result of social media, which have been highlighted in the media in the United Kingdom (UK) and more widely.

This chapter highlights some of the detrimental and positive effects of social media use on children and young people's mental health. The implications for schools, parents, social media and advertising companies and the government are addressed. This chapter highlights that schools cannot solve all of the problems and that other stakeholders also have a responsibility to keep young people safe when they are online.

2. How do young people use social media?

Research suggests that social media use is far more prevalent among young people than older generations [1]. Young people aged 16–24 are the most active social media users with 91% using the internet for social media [1]. Young people use social media for a variety of purposes, including for entertainment, to share information and network with others and to gain support and health information [1].

3. Social media and its links to mental health

Evidence suggests that social media use can result in young people developing conditions including anxiety, stress and depression [1]. There are various reasons for this, and this section will explore the contributing factors. Research has found that four of the five most used social media platforms make young people's feelings of anxiety worse [1]. Research suggests that young people who use social media heavily, i.e., those who spend more than 2 hours per day on social networking sites are more likely to report poor mental health, including psychological distress [2].

Cyber-bullying is a significant problem which affects young people. Evidence suggests that seven in 10 young people experience cyberbullying [1]. Cyberbullying exists in a variety of forms. It can include the posting of hurtful comments online, threats and intimidation towards others in the online space and posting photographs or videos that are intended to cause distress. This is not an exhaustive list. Cyberbullying is fundamentally different to bullying which takes place in person. The victim of the bullying may find it difficult to escape from because it exists within the victim's personal and private spaces such as their homes and bedrooms. Additionally, the number of people witnessing the bullying can be extremely large because of the potential of social media for online posts to be shared across hundreds, thousands and millions of people. For the victim this can be significantly humiliating and result in a loss of confidence and self-worth. Humiliating messages, photographs and videos can be stored permanently online, resulting in the victim repeatedly experiencing the bullying every time they go online. Victims of cyberbullying can experience depression, anxiety, loss of sleep, self-harm and feelings of loneliness [3].

Social media has also been associated with body image concerns. Research indicates that when young girls and women in their teens and early twenties view Facebook for only a short period of time, body image concerns are higher compared to non-users [4]. Young people view images of "ideal" bodies and start to make comparisons with their own bodies. This can result in low body-esteem, particularly if young people feel that their own bodies do not compare favourably to the "perfect" bodies they see online. Young people are heavily influenced by celebrities and may desire to look like them. If they feel that this is unattainable it can result in depression, body-surveillance and low body-confidence. Young people can then start to develop conditions such as eating disorders. The issue of body image is not just a female issue. Young males are also vulnerable and influenced by the muscular, well-toned bodies that they see online. We now live in an age when males are taking increasing interest in their appearance and viewing images of muscular, toned bodies can result in them putting their bodies through extensive fitness regimes and males are also vulnerable to developing eating disorders.

The opportunity for people to use digital editing software to edit their appearance on photographs can also result in young people developing a false sense of beauty. It is worrying that there is a rise in the number of young people seeking to obtain cosmetic surgery [1] and the popularity of "selfies" in recent years has resulted in an increase in images which portray beauty and perfection. These images can have a negative impact on body-esteem and body-confidence.

Research demonstrates that increased social media use has a significant association with poor sleep quality in young people [5]. It seems that young people enjoy being constantly connected to the online world. They develop a "Fear of Missing Out" (FoMO) which is associated with lower mood and lower life satisfaction [6]. This can result in young people constantly checking their devices for messages, even during the night, resulting in broken sleep. Sleep is particularly important during adolescence and broken sleep can result in exhaustion and lack of opportunity for the brain to become refreshed. Lack of sleep quality can have a range of detrimental effects, but it can also impact on school performance and their behaviour. My own conversations with school leaders suggest that many adolescents demonstrate signs of tiredness during the school day. This can result in disengagement in lessons, thus having a detrimental effect on academic attainment.

The link between social media use, self-harm and even suicide is particularly worrying [1]. The fact that young people can access distressing content online that promotes self-harm and suicide is a significant cause for concern. This content attempts to "normalise" self-harm and suicide and can result in young people replicating the actions that they are exposed to.

4. The benefits of social media

Research suggests that young people are increasingly using social media to gain emotional support to prevent and address mental health issues [7]. This is particularly pertinent for young people who represent minority groups, including those who identify as lesbian, gay, bisexual or transgender (LGBT), those with disabilities and those representing black and minority ethnic groups. The use of social media to form online digital communities with others who share similar characteristics can be extremely powerful. Young people from minority groups are able to become "global citizens," thus reducing isolation. Participating in online networks presents them with an opportunity to meet with others who share their identities, to gain mutual support and advice and to gain solidarity. These networks can reduce feelings of loneliness and support the development of a positive, personal identity. They can also support young people to become more resilient to adverse situations which can help them to stay mentally healthy.

While online communities can be beneficial, they also bring associated risks. For example, members of the LGBT networks can become easy targets for abuse, discrimination, harassment and prejudice. It is therefore critical that young people understand how to keep themselves safe online and develop appropriate digital resilience to enable them to address these challenges.

Social media use can allow young people to express themselves positively, letting young people put forward a positive image of themselves [8]. The problem with this is that people tend to use social media to present the best version of themselves and of their lives. This can result in others making unhealthy comparisons between their own lives and the idealised lives that are depicted on the internet, resulting in low self-esteem.

Social media platforms enable young people to share creative content and express their interests and passions with others [1]. This can help to strengthen the development of a positive identity among young people and provide them with numerous opportunities to experiment with a range of interests. This is particularly important for young people who live in rural communities who may find it more challenging to develop social connections in the offline world.

Students living in boarding schools benefit from using social media platforms because it enables them to maintain contact with family members and friends at home. This is particularly important because students living away from home may experience isolation and homesickness and social media platforms facilitate these connections.

Social media platforms offer young people a useful tool to make, maintain or build social connections with others [1]. Additionally, research suggests that strong adolescent friendships can be enhanced by social media interactions [9]. Thus, young people can use social media to cement the friendships that they have formed in the offline world and to develop new friendships that would not have been possible in the offline word due to geographical restrictions.

5. The role of schools

Schools play a critical role in keeping children safe online. A well-planned digital curriculum should cover themes such as digital resilience and digital citizenship so that young people know how to respond to distressing content and how to behave responsibly online. The curriculum should also provide digital literacy skills so that children and young people have the skills to keep their own accounts safe through privacy settings, blocking perpetrators of abuse, reporting abuse and setting passwords. Schools should also support children and young people to critically engage with content they see online. They should be taught to question and interrogate content for accuracy, exploitation, abuse and discrimination.

Schools also play a critical role in developing young people's mental health literacy. This should cover common mental health conditions, including stress, anxiety, depression, self-harm and cyberbullying. Educating young people about mental health is essential and reduces the stigma that has traditionally been associated with mental health conditions. Young people also need to have strategies for managing their own mental health. If their mental health is adversely affected by their experiences online, they need to be taught strategies to self-regulate their emotions and strategies to aid digital resilience. Some young people who have negative experiences online respond by closing down their social media accounts. This situates the control with the perpetrators of abuse and removes control from the victim because they are disadvantaged. Developing practical approaches to aid digital resilience in the face of adversity must be a key component of the digital curriculum that schools provide. Young people need to know how to respond to abuse, who to report it to and how to block the accounts of perpetrators. In addition, they need to be taught about the importance of maintaining secure social media accounts and how to keep themselves safe by not sharing personal information.

Schools need to provide a social need to provide a social media curriculum which is progressive and age appropriate. Given the prevalence of fake content online and content which has been digitally edited, young people need to be taught to critically evaluate content that appears online so that they understand the harmful effects of some content. Themes including exploitation, body-esteem and gender stereotyping can be addressed through critically evaluating online content.

Children and young people often have a good understanding of the issues associated with social media because they are the users of it. Therefore, they experience the issues, sometimes frequently. Working in partnership with young people through empowering them to lead on aspects of social media education is a powerful way of developing student partnership and empowers them to be leaders. Often, young people understand the online applications better than teachers and they are acutely aware of the issues that occur online. Student-led events such as student-led workshops and conferences, which highlight the issues that relate to social media and mental health, are powerful ways of providing ownership to students. Developing digital ambassadors who act as peer mentors to younger students is also a powerful strategy for developing students' confidence and leadership skills. Young people who need someone to talk to about the issues that they are experiencing online can be paired with a digital ambassador who can provide them with confidential advice. Processes for recruiting digital ambassadors would need to be carefully considered by schools and the scheme would need to be properly led and managed by a member of staff to monitor its effectiveness. Student-led peer mentoring schemes are valuable because some students prefer to talk to peers about the issues that they are experiencing rather than teachers or parents.

Schools also play a critical role in educating parents about the relationship between social media and mental health. It is important that parents understand the online applications that their children are using, and schools can play a critical role in developing their understanding. Schools can also provide guidance to parents on the signs and symptoms of mental ill health so that they are better able to identify mental health problems in their child. Schools can provide guidance to parents on how to support their child's mental health at home and guidelines about responsible use of social media in the home. It is critical that parents understand the association between poor sleep quality, mental health and academic attainment and schools can play an important role in this. Schools also play a crucial role in developing parents' knowledge about how to be a good social media role model for their child.

6. The role of other stakeholders

Schools cannot solve the problems associated with social media in isolation. This section outlines the responsibilities of parents, social media companies and advertising companies. The responsibilities of the government are also outlined.

Parents are in a unique position to influence their child's social media use. They should establish clear expectations about the amount of time their child spends online. However, imposing rules on children can lead to conflict and the breakdown of relationships between parents and children. It is far more effective for parents and children to negotiate the rules jointly so that young people have ownership of determining the boundaries of acceptable and unacceptable behaviour. If rules are imposed rather than negotiated it is likely that young people will find ways to break the rules and therefore adopting a top-down approach may not be the most effective way of encouraging young people to develop healthy social media use.

Some parents may try to restrict their child's use of social media by installing filters or by disconnecting the internet supply at specific times of the day or week. However, young people will find ways to subvert this and policing their use of the internet in this way is unlikely to foster digital responsibility. It might be more effective for parents to talk to their child about what it means to be a digitally responsible citizen and to explain why it is important to restrict screen time, particularly during the night. Families might want to consider allocating specific time each day or week when no-one accesses technology.

In addition, parents also need to be role models. They cannot expect their child to demonstrate the skills of digital citizenship and digital responsibility if they are not prepared to demonstrate these skills. It is therefore important for parents to model healthy online behaviours so that their children can then replicate these. It is also important for parents to develop their own digital literacy, so they are aware of the platforms and software that their child is interacting with. Parents also need to develop knowledge of the risks that their children are exposed to, given that these are constantly changing. If parents do not keep abreast of developments, they will not be able to support their child effectively.

Parents should negotiate rules with their children about what constitutes appropriate use of the internet. Imposing rules on children is unlikely to be effective because young people will find ways to resist or subvert these. It is also important that parents provide their children with a degree of autonomy about their internet use. It is unlikely to be helpful if parents continually monitor what their children are doing online. However, it is reasonable for parents to set some rules for appropriate use to protect their child from harm. Examples include:

- not using technology during the night;

- restricting technology use during mealtimes or other social occasions;

- limiting the amount of screen time which children are exposed to.

It will be more effective if young people are involved in discussions with their parents about what might constitute appropriate use of the internet.

Social media companies have a responsibility to protect young people from harm. They can do this in a variety of ways by:

- establishing strict and robust policies on the age at which users can access platforms;

- blocking accounts of perpetrators of abuse;

- reporting abuse to the police;

- removing inappropriate content immediately;

- filtering specific content before it goes live;

- producing information to service users about responsible and safe use of social media;

- generating warning messages when users have exceeded reasonable levels of screen time;

- responding rapidly to reports of abuse.

This is not an exhaustive list. However, it illustrates the sorts of actions that can be adopted by social media companies to protect children and young people from harm. Companies have not responded quickly enough to reports of abuse or inappropriate content as cases of suicide in the UK suggest that social media companies have failed to protect young people from harm. The government also has a clear responsibility to hold companies to account which fail to protect children and young people from harm. Simply fining companies is not enough and will not necessarily address the problem. The government needs to take firmer action against social media companies which breach their safeguarding responsibilities.

In addition, advertising companies have a responsibility to ensure that young people do not develop low body confidence. They can achieve this in a variety of ways. These include:

- providing warning messages that images may have been digitally edited;

- ensuring that images of bodies on products represent a range of body types, including a range of body sizes, disabled bodies and people of colour;

- avoiding gender-stereotypes when advertising products;

- producing warning messages about the dangers associated with product-use so that young people are aware of the risks;

- portraying natural bodies without make-up on some products.

7. Young people's perspectives

Our own research in Cambridge [10] with students in secondary schools demonstrates that they had a good understanding of the benefits and risks associated with social media. Focus groups demonstrated that the students had developed an excellent understanding of the benefits of social media and the relationship between social media use and mental ill health, including sleep deprivation, cyberbullying and low body-esteem. They had also developed a better understanding of how to keep themselves safe online. The quotes and **Figure 1** below are taken from our research report [10].

> *Social media helps you to communicate with your friends if they are far away. It makes you feel good when you get a like on your posts. (Student Y8)*
>
> *You can talk to your friends and family on social media. The disadvantages are that you can get stalked. People can create fake accounts. You can get cyber-bullied. People can hack into other people's accounts and you might not know who is communicating with you. People can become jealous of other people's lives and this can make you sad and depressed. (Student Y9)*
>
> *Some of the pictures can be fake so people can make out that they are leading an exciting life but really, they are not, and this can make others feel worthless. (Student Y8)*
>
> *Social media results in an expectation to show the good part of your life. It can impact on others because they think you are having a good time and they might not be having such a good time. (Student Y9)*

People make mean comments and it makes you feel bad. The bullying can be anonymous, and it reaches a larger audience. You can ignore the insults and carry on with your life. You can report the person or block them. (Student Y9)

Men are expected to be muscular. You get upset because you think "why don't I look like that?" (Student Y8)

I realize that social media has an impact on my sleep. I find it addictive and I am always checking what friends are doing through social media and texting. (Student Y9)

I think online bullying is different to bullying in school. It is easier to say horrible things to someone through social media because you are not saying it to their face. (Student Y8)

We can become stressed through social media because celebrities show images of being slim. This mainly affects women but now men are becoming bothered about how they look. This is stress that becomes a mental health problem. (Student Y9)

You feel you must look as good as celebrity people because people feel you need to be as good looking otherwise you don't get a good reputation. (Student Y8)

Cyber bullying is when you post hateful messages online to directly hurt a person. (Student Y8)

Seeing slim models online (body image) can make your self-esteem feel low. (Student Y8).

The students summarised the advantages and disadvantages of social media below:

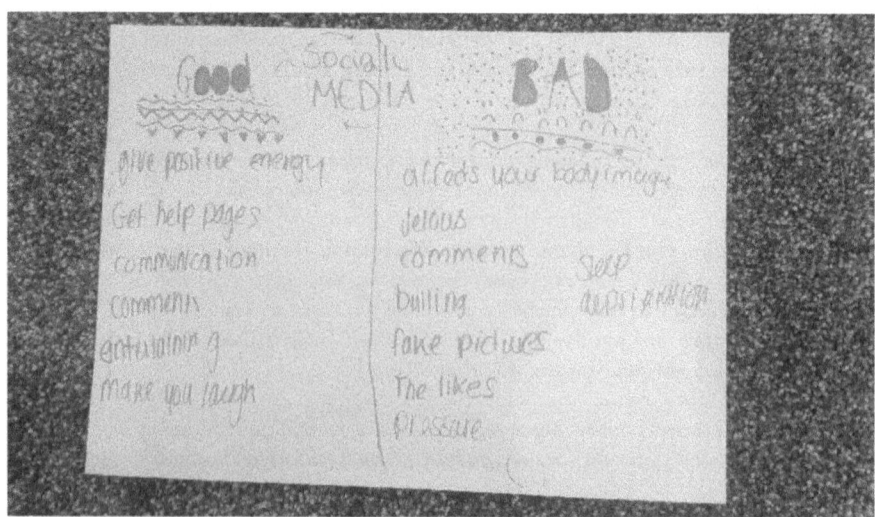

Figure 1.
Students' perspectives on social media.

8. Cyberbullying

Cyberbullying is bullying which takes place in the online world, including bullying which takes place on social media. It takes multiple forms. These include:

- posting hurtful comments;

- posting videos which are targeted directly at a person to cause distress;

- posting photographs which are designed to cause distress;

- inciting others to make hurtful comments aimed at a person;

- sending hurtful text messages using a mobile phone;

- sending hurtful private messages to a person [11].

According to Glazzard and Mitchell [11]:

> *Cyberbullying is fundamentally different to face-to-face bullying in several ways. Firstly, victims cannot escape from it when they are at home because it takes place on mobile phones, tablets and computers. Secondly the abuse is witnessed by a larger audience; messages are in the public domain and can be repeatedly forwarded. This can result in victims experiencing the abuse on multiple occasions, which results in further psychological distress. Thirdly, the evidence of the abuse is usually permanently stored online which means that the abuse is not erased. These messages serve as a permanent reminder of the abuse and this can result in abuse being continually experienced by the victim.*

Forms of cyberbullying are outlined below and taken from Glazzard and Mitchell [11]:

Harassment: Harassment is the act of sending offensive, rude, and insulting messages and being abusive. It includes nasty or degrading comments on posts, photos and in chat rooms and making offensive comments on gaming sites. Posting false and malicious things about people on the internet can be classed as harassment [11].

Denigration: This is when someone may send information about another person that is fake, damaging and untrue. It includes sharing photographs of someone for the purpose to ridicule and spreading fake rumours and gossip. This can be on any site online or on apps. It includes purposely altering photographs of others to ridicule and cause distress [11].

Flaming: Flaming is when someone purposely uses extreme and offensive language and deliberately gets into online arguments and fights. They do this to deliberately cause distress in others [11].

Impersonation: Impersonation is when someone hacks into someone's email or social networking account and uses the person's online identity to send or post vicious or embarrassing material to or about others. It also includes making up fake profiles of others [11].

Outing and trickery: This is when someone shares personal information about someone else or tricks someone into revealing secrets and subsequently forwards it to others. They may also do this with private images and videos too [11].

Cyberstalking: Cyberstalking is the act of repeatedly sending messages that include threats of harm, harassment, intimidating messages, or engaging in other online activities that make a person afraid for their safety. The actions may be illegal depending on what they are doing. Cyberstalking can take place on the internet or via mobile 'phones. Examples include:

- silent calls;

- insulting and threatening texts;

- abusive verbal messages;

- cases of stolen identities [11]

Exclusion: This is when others intentionally leave someone out of a group such as group messages, online apps, gaming sites and other online engagement. This is also a form of social bullying and is very common [11].

Bullying by spreading rumours and gossip: Online abuse, rumours and gossip can go viral very quickly and be shared by many people within several minutes. It is not uncommon for former close friends or partners to share personal secrets about victims [11].

Threatening behaviour: Threatening behaviour which is directed at a victim to cause alarm and distress is a criminal offence. Taking screenshots of the evidence and reporting it is one way of challenging this [11].

Happy slapping: This is an incident where a person is assaulted while other people take photographs or videos on their mobile phones. The pictures or videos are then circulated by mobile phone or uploaded on the internet [11].

Grooming: Grooming is when someone builds an emotional connection with a child to gain their trust for the purposes of abuse and exploitation. It is conducted by strangers (or new "friends") and may include:

- pressurising someone to do something they do not wish to do;

- making someone take their clothes off;

- pressurising someone to engage in sexual conversations;

- pressurising someone to take naked photographs of themselves;

- making someone engage in sexual activity via the internet [11].

Groomers may spend a long time establishing a "relationship" with the victim by using the following strategies:

- pretending to be someone they are not, for example, saying they are the same age online;

- offering advice or understanding;

- buying gifts;

- giving the child attention;

- using their professional position or reputation;

- giving compliments;

- taking them on trips, outings or holidays [11].

Inappropriate images: It is very easy to save any pictures of anyone on any site and upload them to the internet. Uploading pictures of someone to cause distress is a form of cyberbullying. This also includes digitally altering pictures to embarrass someone [11].

Bystander effect: Witnessing cyberbullying and doing nothing about it is not acceptable. Some people are worried about getting involved but victims of bullying need brave witnesses to make a stand. Perpetrators of bullying thrive when they have an audience. Making a stand against what they are doing is an important way to reduce their power. Most sites now operate a reporting facility so that online abuse can be reported and addressed. Bystanders are not innocent. They have a responsibility to report abuse that they witness [11].

9. Technoference

The following text is taken from our blog [12].

Research from Queensland University of Technology has identified that half of young people aged 18–24 are less productive and more tired because of their mobile phones. Scientists have adopted the term "technoference" to describe the way that mobile phones intrude on and interrupt everyday conversations and the way they interrupt other aspects of people's daily lives.

It is worrying that family life is being interrupted by technology. While technology has significant benefits, continual use of technology can impact detrimentally on the quality of people's interactions and conversations. We live in a society where people are constantly attached to their technology. People interact with technology on public transport, in meetings and during leisure time rather than engaging in productive, meaningful conversations. It seems that people would rather interact with a phone rather than having a conversation and while this is not necessarily a problem in some contexts, it can have a negative impact in other contexts. For example, young children require social interaction with adults. This allows them to develop secure attachments with significant others, it enables them to learn about the world and through conversation children are exposed to language. Exposure to language underpins reading and writing development. Children who have rich exposure to language become better readers, better writers and understand far better what they are reading. Lack of exposure to language can impact detrimentally on the structure of the brain. This can create reading difficulties and even lead to difficulties which are consistent with dyslexia, even though the difficulties may not have a genetic origin. The brain is malleable. It is responsive to environmental influences and lack of exposure to language can impact on phonological and phonemic awareness. Both of these skills play a critical role in reading development. Interacting with technology can restrict opportunities for communication between babies, children and their parents and can interrupt the flow of normal conversation.

It would appear that adolescents seem to be attached to their phones during the night. They are desperate to network and keep up-to-date with their online peers. This results in broken sleep and tiredness during the school day. Adolescents need approximately 8–10 hours sleep but our research demonstrates that some get as little as 2 hours sleep. These students attend school in a state of exhaustion. They are too tired to concentrate and it affects their learning and their behaviour. Disengagement in lessons results in them falling behind in their schoolwork and they then develop other problems such as low confidence and low self-worth.

Real-time social connections are vital for positive wellbeing. Schools play a key role in teaching young people about how to stay healthy and in particular, the need for sleep. However, parents also play a critical role in supporting young people to develop positive habits through setting boundaries. Examples of boundaries might include restricting access to technology in bedrooms and at mealtimes. Also, parents need to be good role models by ensuring that they do not allow technology to interrupt conversations and other daily experiences.

10. Statistics

Statistics demonstrate the risks of internet use on young people's lives. Key statistics are summarised below [13]:

- year on year increases in the numbers and rates of police-recorded online child sexual offences in England and Wales and Northern Ireland

- increases in police-recorded offences of obscene publications or indecent photos in all four UK nations over the last 5 years

- increases in the number of URLs confirmed by the Internet Watch Foundation (IWF) as containing child sexual abuse imagery since 2015

- less than half of children aged 12–15 say they know how to change their settings to control who can view their social media

- the majority of parents, carers and members of the public agree that social networks should have a legal responsibility to keep children safe on their platforms.

Additionally:

- a total of 5161 crimes of sexual communication with a child have been recorded in 18 months [14];

- in 2019 there has been almost a 50% increase in offence in offences recorded in latest 6 months compared to same period in previous year [14];

- in 2010 there has been a 200% rise in recorded instances in the use of Instagram to target and abuse children over the same time period [14];

- there have been over 5000 online grooming offences recorded in 18 months [14].

11. Conclusions

Social media use can have a detrimental impact on children and young people's mental health. It can result in anxiety, depression, body image concerns, self-harm, substance abuse and even death. However, for young people social media is a tool for networking, keeping in touch with friends, exchanging information, a source of support and advice and a rich source of knowledge. Preventing children and young people from using social media is not an appropriate solution, given all the benefits that come with it. Schools, parents and the digital industry need to do all they can to keep children safe from harm through adopting a proactive approach rather than a reactive approach when crises occur.

Acknowledgements

We wish to thank Leeds Beckett University and the Carnegie Centre of Excellence for Mental Health in Schools for facilitating this research.

Conflict of interest

The authors declare no conflict of interest.

Author details

Jonathan Glazzard* and Samuel Stones
Leeds Beckett University, Leeds, UK

*Address all correspondence to: j.glazzard@leedsbeckett.ac.uk

IntechOpen

© 2019 The Author(s). Licensee IntechOpen. This chapter is distributed under the terms of the Creative Commons Attribution License (http://creativecommons.org/licenses/by/3.0), which permits unrestricted use, distribution, and reproduction in any medium, provided the original work is properly cited.

References

[1] Royal Society for Public Health (RSPH). #Status of Mind Social media and young people's mental health and wellbeing. RSPH; 2017

[2] Sampasa-Kanyinga H, Lewis RF. Frequent use of social networking sites is associated with poor psychological functioning among children and adolescents. Cyberpsychology, Behavior and Social Networking. 2015;**18**(7): 380-385. DOI: 10.1089/cyber.2015.0055

[3] Stop Bullying.gov. Effects of Bullying. 2017. Available from: https://www.stopbullying.gov/at-risk/effects/ [Accessed: 17 April]

[4] Tiggeman M, Slater A. The internet and body image concerns in preteenage girls. The Journal of Early Adolescents. 2013;**34**(5):606-620. DOI: 10.1177/0272431613501083

[5] Scott H, Gardani M, Biello S, Woods H. Social Media Use, Fear of Missing Out and Sleep Outcomes in Adolescents. 2016. Available from: https://www.researchgate.net/publication/308903222_Social_media_use_fear_of_missing_out_and_sleep_outcomes_in_adolescence [Accessed: 17 April]

[6] Pryzbylski A, Murayama K, DeHaan C, Gladwell V. Motivational, emotional and behavioural correlates of fear of missing out. Computers in Human Behaviour. 2013;**29**(4): 1841-1848. DOI: 10.1016/j.chb.2013.02.014

[7] Farnan JM, Snyder SL, Worster BK, et al. Online medical professionalism: Patient and public relationships: Policy statement from the American College of Physicians and the Federation of State Medical Boards. Annals of Internal Medicine. 2013;**158**(8):620-662

[8] University of Minnesota- Introduction to Psychology. 6.3 Adolescents: Developing Independence and Identity. Available from: http://open.lib.umn.edu/intropsyc/chapter/6-3-adolescence-developing-independence-and-identity/ [Accessed: 17 April]

[9] Lenhart A. Chapter 4: Social Media and Friendships. 2015. Available from: http://www.pewinternet.org/2015/08/06/chapter-4-social-media-and-friendships/ [Accessed: 17 April]

[10] Cambridge United Community Trust/Leeds Beckett University. Mind Your Head-Programme Evaluation. Available from: https://leedsbeckett.ac.uk/-/media/files/School-of-Education/mind_your_head_evaluation_report.pdf

[11] Glazzard J, Mitchell C. Social Media and Mental Health in Schools. St Albans: Critical Publishing; 2018

[12] Glazzard J, Stones S. Technoference. Leeds Beckett University; 2019. Available from: https://www.leedsbeckett.ac.uk/blogs/carnegie-education/2019/04/technoference/

[13] National Society for the Protection of Cruelty to Children (NSPCC). Available from: https://learning.nspcc.org.uk/research-resources/how-safe-are-our-children/

[14] National Society for the Protection of Cruelty to Children (NSPCC). Available from: https://www.nspcc.org.uk/what-we-do/news-opinion/over-5000-grooming-offences-recorded-18-months/

Chapter 3

Parent-Child Interaction Therapy: Theory and Research to Practice

Perrine Heymann, Brynna H. Heflin and Daniel M. Bagner

Abstract

This chapter will focus on the theory behind and research on Parent-Child Interaction Therapy (PCIT), a treatment developed for young children with disruptive behavior problems. We will describe and provide details about PCIT, which is based on both attachment and social learning models, and incorporates an innovative approach to treatment in which therapists coach caregivers "live" via a wireless headset while each caregiver interacts with their child. In addition, we will review research that has examined PCIT with a variety of diverse populations (e.g., children with developmental delay, physical abuse histories, anxiety and depression, and children from underrepresented racial and ethnic minority families), settings (e.g., clinic, home, school) and formats (e.g., individual, group, intensive). Finally, we will present a case study of PCIT with a child younger than 2 years to demonstrate the effectiveness of PCIT and highlight some common challenges and pitfalls that clinicians may face in clinical practice.

Keywords: early childhood, externalizing behavior, behavior parent training, parent-child interaction therapy

1. Introduction

Externalizing behavior problems, which include behaviors such as physical aggression (e.g., throwing and hitting), defiance (e.g., not complying to parents demands), hyperactivity and impulsivity, and tantrums are one of the leading causes for referring young children to a mental health professional [1]. When these externalizing behaviors become functionally impairing, interfere with everyday life tasks (e.g., going to the grocery store or eating at restaurants), and persist across multiple settings, they may represent a clinically elevated problem. It is important to note that most young children exhibit these behaviors to some degree, and it is only when these behaviors are persistent and interfere with daily functioning that they warrant intervention. Young children with externalizing behavior problems are at elevated risk for more severe behavior problems later in development [2], academic difficulties [3, 4], and substance use and criminality [5]. Additionally, parents of these children are more likely to display higher levels of stress [6] and other mental health concerns, such as depression and anxiety [7–9], compared to parents of children without externalizing behavior problems.

2. Theory for the development of externalizing behavior problems in young children

There are different theories on how early externalizing behavior problems develop. For example, in attachment theory [10], infants use their parents as a secure base to explore their environment, and the extent to which parents are sensitive and responsive in this relationship is associated with the infant's socialization [10, 11]. Based on this model, infants are at increased risk for externalizing behavior problems if they have an insecure attachment with their parent and their parent lacks warmth [12–14]. Thus, attachment-based interventions focus on enhancing the parent-child relationship. One example of an attachment-based intervention is the Video-Feedback Intervention to Promote Positive Parenting (VIPP [15]), which was developed to reinforce parents' sensitive responsiveness to their infant. During sessions, parents are videotaped interacting with their child. These video-taped interactions are used to give feedback to the parent about interactions highlighting moments of empathy and sensitivity. VIPP has been shown to improve parent responsiveness and reduce externalizing behavior problems but has not been shown to change infant attachment classification [16, 17].

Social learning is another theory informing how behavior problems may develop in young children and suggests young children learn behaviors through observation and function as a result of reinforcement and punishment by parents [18]. Specifically, according to Patterson's [19] coercive cycle, children and parents both negatively reinforce negative behaviors in one another. For example, imagine a child in a supermarket who wants a candy bar, but their parent sets a limit by saying no. The child may throw a temper tantrum until the parent removes the limit and gives the child the candy, thereby negatively reinforcing the child's tantrum. Similarly, the parent might yell at the child for the tantrum, which may stop as a result, and thereby reinforce the parent's yelling.

Behavioral parent-training interventions integrate attachment and social learning theories and focus on improving the parent-child relationship while teaching parents to use effective discipline strategies. These behavioral parent-training interventions emerged from Dr. Constance "Connie" Hanf's model, which targets improvements in parent-child interactions (Hanf-Model [20]). A systematic review of psychosocial interventions for disruptive behavior disorders suggests these behavioral parent-training interventions have strong support from studies examining their efficacy [21] and include programs such as the Incredible Years (IY [22]), Helping the Non-Compliant Child (HNC [23]), Triple P—Positive Parenting Program (PPP [24]) and Parent Child Interaction Therapy (PCIT [25]). Although these behavioral parent-training programs share commonalities, each program has unique components. For the remainder of this chapter we will focus on PCIT.

3. Parent-child interaction therapy (PCIT)

PCIT, developed by Dr. Sheila Eyberg, is an evidenced-based, manualized treatment for young children with behavior problems that stems from the principles of play therapy [25]. In PCIT, the overall goal is to enhance the parent-child relationship through active and live coaching of the parent during interactions with the child. For instance, in clinic-based PCIT, the parent and child are in a play room, while the therapist coaches the parent through a one-way mirror with the use of a "bug in their ear" or wireless headset device. PCIT consists of two phases: the Child-Directed Interaction (CDI) and the Parent-Directed Interaction (PDI). At the beginning of both of these phases, parents participate in a teach session during which the clinician discusses the different skills that will be used during each phase of treatment. The following sessions are coach sessions, where the clinician coaches the parent while they interact with their child.

During the CDI phase, the therapist teaches and coaches the parent in their use of the PRIDE skills to follow the child's lead in the play and to enhance their relationship. The P in PRIDE stands for Praise. Specifically, the therapist coaches the parent to use specific (i.e., labeled) praises to reinforce specific appropriate behaviors (e.g., I love how you are playing so gently with the toys). The R in PRIDE stands for Reflection, which refers to repeating the child's appropriate vocalizations and verbalizations. For example, if the child says, "Cup" the parent is encouraged to repeat (and expand upon) the child's verbalization with a response such as, "That is a red cup." Reflections that provide additional information may help the child expand their vocabulary. The I in PRIDE stands for Imitation, which refers to copying and expanding on the child's play. For example, if the child is building a house with blocks the parent is coached to also build a house with blocks and possibly add a garage out of blocks. The D in PRIDE stands for Description, which involves a parent using a running commentary of their child's ongoing behavior (e.g., "You are putting the blue block on top of the red block") and may help keep the child engaged in play. The E in PRIDE stands for Enjoyment because it is important for parents to have fun and be enthusiastic while playing with their child to keep their child engaged.

In addition to using the PRIDE skills, therapists instruct parents to avoid commands, questions, and criticisms. Commands can be direct (e.g., Give me the block) or indirect (e.g., "Let's play with the cars") and lead the play by suggesting what the child should do. Similarly, questions at times can be hidden commands (e.g., Would you clean up the toys?) and can also take the lead in the conversation between the parent and child. Questions and commands can place a demand on the child to respond or comply with their parents, which can lead to the coercive cycle and make the play less enjoyable for the child and parent. It is important to note that questions and commands can help children learn in some contexts (e.g., reading) but can be counterproductive during child-directed play, such as CDI. The last thing clinicians instruct parents to avoid are criticisms or negative statements about the child or pointing out mistakes the child made. Criticisms can make the interaction less enjoyable and lower a child's self-esteem.

During the CDI phase, therapists also coach parents to use active ignoring, which is when parents remove attention from the child for inappropriate or annoying behaviors (e.g., tantrums, whining). The combination of positive attention (i.e., PRIDE skills) when the child engages in positive behaviors with the removal of attention for negative behaviors helps the child learn to engage in more positive behaviors for attention. It is recommended that parents practice using the PRIDE skills for 5 minutes every day during "special time" with their child to improve their skills and their child's behavior. Recommended toys for special time include construction toys (e.g., blocks, Legos), pretend play toys (e.g., dolls, farm animals), and creative toys (e.g., coloring). Toys and games to avoid are those with specific rules (e.g., board games), that make messes (e.g., paint, playdough), or that lead to aggressive behaviors (e.g., balls, superhero figures). During treatment sessions, therapists monitor special time practice and skill acquisition.

During the PDI phase, parents learn to lead the play and use limit setting to increase child compliance. Specifically, therapists teach parents to use specific and direct commands and follow-through with consistent consequences. The parent starts the PDI sequence by giving their child a direct command. If the child complies within a five second interval, the parent provides the child with a labeled praise (e.g., thank you so much for listening the first time). If the child does not comply to the command after 5 seconds, the parent gives the child a warning indicating that if they do not comply they will have to go to the timeout chair. If the child complies after the warning, the parent gives the child a labeled praise. However, if the child does not comply, the parent tells the child that they did not listen so they have to go to the timeout chair, which is an adult-sized chair facing a corner or wall to minimize distractions. After 3 minutes and when the child has been quiet for 5 seconds, the parent restates the original command. If the child does not comply, they go back to the time out chair, and the sequence starts over until the child complies. In the event the child does not stay on the timeout chair, a back-up room is used when the child gets off the chair. The child is brought to the room for 1 minute and then returned to the chair.

The PDI sequence is first practiced during play for both the parent and child to learn the routine. Once parents feel comfortable using these skills on their own, they are encouraged to use the PDI sequence throughout the day and eventually establish standing house rules (e.g., no yelling) for which the child will automatically go to the timeout chair without a warning. The PDI sequence is first practiced in the home, however, once parents feel comfortable using PDI, they are coached and encouraged to use it in public settings. The therapist works with the parents to adapt the sequence in different public settings (e.g., grocery store).

PCIT is a time unlimited treatment, but the average length of treatment ranges from 12 to 14 weekly sessions, each lasting approximately 1 hour [26]. Graduation from treatment termination requires parents to master skills learned during treatment and that the child's behavior is within normal limits. To meet mastery criteria for CDI, parents must use 10 labeled praises, 10 reflections, 10 behavior descriptions, and less than 3 questions, commands, and criticisms during a 5-minute child-directed play. To meet mastery criteria for PDI, parents must use direct commands and follow through the sequence effectively 75% of the time. To monitor the child's disruptive behavior throughout treatment, parents complete the Eyberg Child Behavior Inventory (ECBI [27]) weekly prior to each session. The ECBI's clinical cut-off score helps indicate when a child's behavior is no longer clinically significant compared to peers' behavior.

4. Efficacy of PCIT

PCIT has been found to be effective in reducing child externalizing behavior problems, as well as increasing child compliance, enhancing the parent child relationship, and reducing parenting stress [28, 29]. In addition to children with externalizing behavior problems, PCIT and adaptations of PCIT have been shown to be effective with other at-risk child populations, such as children with early developmental or neurodevelopmental delays [30–33], anxiety [34–36], and depression [37, 38]. PCIT also has been shown to be effective in increasing maternal sensitivity and positive interactions in parents at risk for maltreatment and abuse [39, 40], as well as in children and families from ethnically and racially diverse backgrounds, such as Puerto Rican [41], Mexican-American [42, 43], Alaskan native [44], Chinese [45], and Norweigan families [46] to name a few.

In addition to targeting diverse populations, PCIT has been shown to be effective when delivered in different formats. For example, research has demonstrated that PCIT can be delivered effectively in a group format [47–49], in which three to six families practice the skills and provide feedback to one another. Additionally, research has demonstrated feasibility of intensive versions of PCIT [50, 51], in which treatment is condensed into 2 weeks. Furthermore, adaptations of PCIT have been delivered in school settings with teachers [52, 53] and in the families' homes [54–56], including a brief, in-home adaptation of PCIT for infants ages

12–15 months from high-risk families [57]. Research on this adaptation, called the Infant Behavior Program (IBP), has demonstrated that infants randomized to the IBP displayed lower levels of externalizing behavior problems through a 6-month follow-up compared to infants in a standard care pediatric primary care group. Additionally, in comparison to infants in the control group, infants who received the IBP demonstrated increases in language that were mediated by changes in infant behavior [58] and parenting behavior [59, 60]. For illustrative purposes, we describe below a fictional case study based on experiences with actual PCIT cases.

5. Case example

"Matthew" was a 22-month-old Hispanic boy who lived with his 7-year-old sister, 8-year-old brother, and biological mother, who reported an annual income of $22,200. Matthew's mother came to the clinic after his primary care physician recommended treatment for Matthew's aggressive behaviors. Matthew's mother reported that he frequently bites his older sister and brother, as well as other children at daycare, and that he can be destructive with his toys (e.g., throws toys at others). Additionally, Matthew's mother reported that when Matthew becomes upset, he has difficulty responding to his mother's instructions and demands. His primary care physician as well as his mother also reported delays in Mathew's expressive speech.

At an evaluation, results revealed clinically elevated scores on the externalizing and dysregulation domains on the Infant-Toddler Social-Emotional Assessment (ITSEA [61]), as well as on the activity/impulsivity, aggression/defiance, negative emotionality, compliance, and attention subscales. He also demonstrated delayed speech, as reported by his mother and physician, and as demonstrated in his scores on the expressive communication subscale on the Preschool Language Scales, Fifth Edition (PLS-5 [62]). Matthew's mother endorsed clinically significant symptoms of disruptive behavior on the ECBI [63], with a score of 146 (T-score = 64) on the Intensity Scale. Matthew's mother's scores at baseline also revealed clinically significant levels on the Parental Distress and difficult child subscales of the Parenting Stress Index, Fourth Edition (PSI-4 [64]), as well as clinically significant levels of depressive symptoms on the Center for Epidemiologic Studies Depression Scale (CES-D [65]). During the evaluation, Matthew displayed frequent aggressive and defiant behaviors in the evaluation setting and used limited communication.

As a result of the evaluation, Matthew's mother was recommended to receive PCIT in order to learn effective skills to manage Matthew's externalizing behavior problems and improve her relationship and interactions with Matthew. An in-home PCIT program was recommended for the family, as difficulties made traveling to the clinic for treatment very difficult. The family completed ten sessions of in-home PCIT, which included one CDI teach and five CDI coach sessions, as well as one PDI teach and three PDI coach sessions, over 4 months. The family attended PCIT sessions consistently until the PDI-phase of treatment, during which time the family's attendance decreased due to work schedule changes and health difficulties in the extended family.

During the CDI phase of treatment, Matthew's mother used several questions and commands. The therapist, who was a doctoral student in clinical psychology, coached Matthew's mother to use the PRIDE skills, with an initial focus on labeled praises and by prompting Matthew's mother with statements such as, "Tell him exactly what he did a great job doing." With coaching and consistent practice using labeled praises and other PRIDE skills over the first five CDI sessions, Matthew's mother increased her use of labeled praises (from 0 in CDI Coach 1 to 10 in CDI Coach 5) and behavior descriptions (from 0 in CDI Coach 1 to 11 in CDI Coach 5). Additionally, while there were not many opportunities to reflect Matthew given his limited speech, Matthew's mother reflected his sounds (e.g., "choo choo" for a train) consistently throughout the CDI sessions. She decreased the number of questions and commands used during sessions, in addition to continuing to avoid critical language. By the end of the five CDI sessions, Matthew's mother reported increased engagement in the parent-child interaction, as well as an increase in Matthew's speech.

During the PDI phase of treatment, the therapist coached Matthew's mother to use effective direct commands. During the first PDI session, Matthew was unable to stay on the chair for the full 3 minutes, and went back and forth between the chair and the time-out room five times. During this sequence, Matthew was very dysregulated, as he yelled, screamed, and kicked his mother when she moved him from the chair to the room each time. By PDI Coach 3, he was able to stay on the chair for the full 3 minutes without yelling or jumping off. By PDI Coach 3, Matthew quickly complied with his mother's commands and no longer went to the timeout chair or room. As displayed in **Figure 1**, Matthew's scores on the ECBI Intensity Scale dropped and stayed below the clinical range after the CDI Coach 5 session and continued to show improvement throughout the PDI phase of treatment.

Immediately following treatment, Matthew demonstrated clinically significant decreases in parent-reported externalizing behavior problems and aggressive behaviors at home. Specifically, at post-treatment, Matthew's score on the ECBI Intensity Scale was a 111, which was a 35-point drop from his pre-treatment score and within the normal range (T-score = 54). Additionally, Matthew's mother reported fewer temper tantrums throughout the day and increased compliance to commands, as well as increased spontaneous speech at home. Relatedly, Matthew's speech improved over the course of treatment as documented by his increased score on the PLS-5 expressive communication subscale from pre-treatment (standard score = 63) to post-treatment (standard score = 79).

In addition to changes in child behavior, Matthew's mother demonstrated improvements in her own skills from pre to post-treatment. As displayed in **Figure 2**, Matthew's mother demonstrated increases in do skills and decreases in don't skills. Furthermore, she reached mastery criteria (i.e., 10 behavior descriptions, 10 reflections, and 10 labeled praises, as well as less than 3 questions, commands and criticisms, during a 5-minute child-directed play) before the end of CDI, and continued to demonstrate excellent use of the skills through the end of PDI. Matthew's mother did not reach mastery criteria for PDI, and Mathew was compliant to about 60% his mother's commands, most (80%) of which were directly stated. Additionally, Matthew's mother reported lower levels of parenting

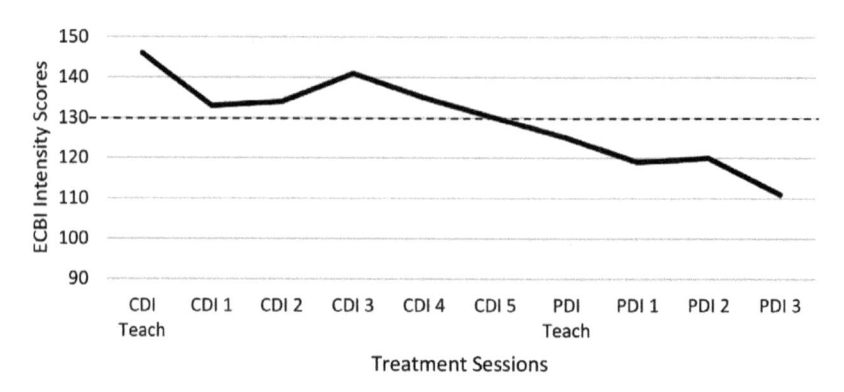

Figure 1.
ECBI Intensity Scale scores across treatment. Note: The above graph shows the decrease in ECBI intensity score, as reported by Matthew's mother, over the course of the 10 sessions.

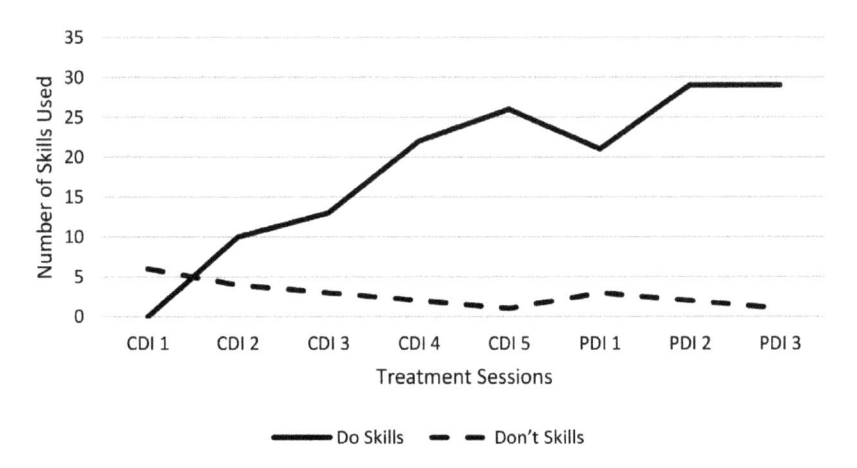

Figure 2.
"Do" and "don't" maternal skills across treatment.

stress related to stress in the parent-child relationship. However, her depressive symptoms remained in the clinically significant range and appropriate referrals for follow-up treatment for the mother were provided.

At a 6-month follow-up, parent-reported externalizing behavior problems and aggressive behaviors remained in the subclinical range, with a score of 110, which was consistent with his score at post-treatment (score = 111) and were still significantly lower than scores on the ECBI at baseline (score = 146). Matthew's mother also reported that Matthew rarely bit his older sister or threw toys and complied to commands quickly. She stated that he continues to remain very engaged in activities with her when she uses the PRIDE skills, which has further facilitated her motivation to continue using the skills learned during treatment. Finally, while Matthew continued to have a speech delay, his speech-pathologist indicated that his scores continued to improve since post-treatment.

Ultimately, in-home PCIT was an effective treatment for this child in reducing his externalizing behavior problems and increasing language production. The family was able to attend a number of sessions, but only attended 3 PDI sessions. It is possible that after the child's behaviors decreased, the family felt less motivated to continue treatment as the behaviors appeared to be more manageable. However, the family may have benefited from additional coaching in the time-out sequence in PDI to maximize the long-term benefits and learning of the sequence. Additionally, despite the demonstrated positive changes in child behavior and parental skill use, maternal depressive symptoms continued to be a challenge for the mother, which also may have impacted attendance during the second phase of treatment. Providing resources for parents experiencing depressive symptomatology or high levels of stress may be an appropriate supplement to parent-child treatment, and may increase parental likelihood of engagement. Despite these challenges, children from low-income, single-parent households have barriers to treatment participation, such as lack of transportation, so the in-home PCIT treatment approach may be a useful approach to reach these families.

6. Conclusion

In summary, young children with externalizing behavior problems are at elevated risk for future difficulties with academics, peer relationships, and continued behavior problems. Research has demonstrated that behavioral parenting interventions, such as PCIT, can be effective in reducing externalizing behavior problems in young children across a variety of settings (e.g., clinic, school, in home). As demonstrated in the fictional case study above, PCIT adaptations, such as in-home sessions, can be effective in reducing aggressive and non-compliant behaviors, as well as increasing child language productivity and rippling effects such as decreasing parental stress. For further information on PCIT and information on how to receive training and become certified in PCIT, please visit the PCIT International website (www.pcit.org).

Author details

Perrine Heymann*, Brynna H. Heflin and Daniel M. Bagner
Florida International University, Miami, FL, United States

*Address all correspondence to: pheymann@fiu.edu

IntechOpen

© 2020 The Author(s). Licensee IntechOpen. This chapter is distributed under the terms of the Creative Commons Attribution License (http://creativecommons.org/licenses/by/3.0), which permits unrestricted use, distribution, and reproduction in any medium, provided the original work is properly cited.

References

[1] Kazdin AE. Psychotherapy for children and adolescents. Annual Review of Psychology. 2003;**54**:253-276. DOI: 54.101601.145105

[2] Shaw DS, Gilliom M, Ingoldsby EM, Nagin DS. Trajectories leading to school-age conduct problems. Developmental Psychology. 2003;**39**:189-200. DOI: 10.1037/0012-1649.39.2.189

[3] Gilliam WS. Prekindergarteners Left behind: Expulsion Rates in State Prekindergarten Systems. New Haven, CT: Yale Child Studies Center; 2005

[4] Van Lier PAC, Vitaro F, Barker ED, Brendgen M, Tremblay RE, Boivin M. Peer victimization, poor academic achievement, and the link between childhood externalizing and internalizing problems. Child Development. 2012;**83**:1775-1788. DOI: 10.1111/j.1467-8624.2012.01802

[5] Petersen IT, Bates JE, Dodge KA, Lansford JE, Pettit GS. Describing and predicting developmental profiles of externalizing problems from childhood to adulthood. Development and Psychopathology. 2015;**27**:791-818. DOI: 10.1017/S0954579414000789

[6] Briggs-Gowan MJ, Carter AS, Skuban EM, Horwitz SM. Prevalence of social-emotional and behavioral problems in a community sample of 1- and 2- year-old children. Journal of the American Academy of Child and Adolescent Psychiatry. 2001;**40**:811-818. DOI: 10.1097/00004583-200107000-00016

[7] Downey G, Coyne J. Children of depressed parents: An integrative review. Psychological Bulletin. 1990;**108**:50-76. DOI: 10.1037/0033-2909.108.1.50

[8] Faught J, Bierl C, Barton B, Kemp A. Stress in mothers of young children with eczema. Archives of Disease in Childhood. 2007;**92**:683-686. DOI: 10.1136/adc.2006.112268

[9] Pauli-Pott U, Darui A, Beckmann D. Infants with atopic dermatitis: Maternal hopelessness, child-rearing attitudes and perceived infant temperament. Psychotherapy and Psychosomatics. 1999;**68**:39-45. DOI: 10.1159/000012309

[10] Bowlby J. Attachment and Loss, Attachment (Rev. Ed.). Vol. 1. Harmondsworth, England: Penguin; 1969

[11] Ainsworth MDS, Blehar MC, Waters E, Wall S. Patterns of Attachment: A Psychological Study of the Strange Situation. Hillsdale, NJ: Erlbaum; 1978

[12] Belsky J, Woodworth S, Crnic K. Trouble in the second year: Three questions about family interaction. Child Development. 1996;**67**:556-578. DOI: 10.1111/j.1467-8624.1996.tb01751.x

[13] Greenberg MT, Speltz ML, DeKlyen M, Endriga MC. Attachment security in preschoolers with and without externalizing behavior problems: A replication. Development and Psychopathology. 1991;**3**:413-430. DOI: 10.1017/S0954579400007604

[14] Olson SL, Bates JE, Sandy JM, Lanthier R. Early developmental precursors of externalizing behavior in middle childhood and adolescence. Journal of Abnormal Child Psychology. 2001;**28**:119-133. DOI: 10.1023/A:1005166629744

[15] Juffer F, Bakermans-Kranenburg MJ, van Ijzendoorn MH. Introduction and outline of the VIPP and VIPP-R program. In: Juffer F, Bakmans-Kranenburg MJ, van Ijzendoorn MH, editors. Promoting Positive Parenting: An

Attachment-Based Intervention. Mahwah, NJ: Erlbaum; 2008

[16] Klein Velderman M, Bakermans-Kranenburg MJ, Juffer F, van Ijzendoorn MH. Effects of attachment-based interventions on maternal sensitivity and infant attachment: Differential susceptibility of highly reactive infants. Journal of Family Psychology. 2016;20:266-274. DOI: 10.1037/0893-3200.20.2.266

[17] Kalinauskiene L, Cekuoliene D, van Ijzendoorn MH, Bakermans-Kranenburg MJ, Juffer F, Kusakovskaja I. Supporting insensitive mothers: The Vilnius randomized control trail of video-feedback intervention to promote maternal sensitivity and infant attachment security. Child, Health and Development. 2009;35:613-624. DOI: 10.1111/j.1365-2214.2009.00962

[18] Bandura A. Social Learning Theory. Morristown, NJ: General Learning Press; 1977

[19] Patterson GR. The aggressive child: Victim and architect of a coercive system. In: Mash E, Hamerlynck L, Handy L, editors. Behavior Modification and Families: Theory and Research. New York: Brunner/Mazel; 1978. pp. 131-158

[20] Reitman D, McMahon RJ. Constance "Connie" Hanf (1917-2002): The mentor and the model. Cogntive and Behavioral Practice. 2013;20:106-116. DOI: 10.1016/j.cbpra.2012.02.005

[21] Eyberg SM, Nelson MM, Boggs SR. Evidence-based psychosocial treatments for children and adolescents with disruptive behavior. Journal of Clinical Child and Adolescent Psychology. 2008;37:1-23. DOI: 10.1080/15374410701820117

[22] Webster-Stratton C, Reid MJ. The incredible years parents, teachers, and children's training series: A multifaceted approach for young children with conduct disorder. In: Weisz JR, Kazdin AE, editors. Evidence-Based Psychotherapies for Children and Adolescents. New York: Guilford Press; 2010

[23] McMahon RJ, Forehand RL. Helping the Noncompliant Child: Family-Based Treatment for Oppositional Behavior. 2nd ed. New York: Guilford Press; 2003

[24] Sanders MR, Cann W, Markie-Dadds C. The triple P—positive parenting programme: A universal population-level approach to the prevention of child abuse. Child Abuse Review. 2003;12:155-171. DOI: 10.1002/car.798

[25] Zisser A, Eyberg SM. Treating oppositional behavior in children using parent-child interaction therapy. Evidence-based Psychotherapies for Children and Adolescents. 2010;2:179-193

[26] Thomas R, Zimmer-Gembeck MJ. Behavioral outcomes of parent-child interaction therapy and triple P- positive parenting programe: A review and meta-analysis. Journal of Abnormal and Child Psychology. 2007;35:475-495. DOI: 10.1007/s10802-007-9104-9

[27] Eyberg SM, Pincus D. Eyberg Child Behavior Inventory and Sutter-Eyberg Student Behavior Inventory—Revised. Odessa, FL: Psychological Assessment Resources; 1999

[28] Nixon RDV, Sweeney L, Erickson DB, Touyz SW. Parent-child interaction therapy: A comparison of standard and abbreviated treatments for oppositional defiant preschoolers. Journal of Consulting and Clinical Psychology. 2003;71:251-260. DOI: 10.1037/0022-006X.71.2.251

[29] Schuhmann EM, Foote RC, Eyberg SM, Boggs SR, Algina J. Efficacy of parent-child interaction therapy: Interim report of a

randomized trail with short-term maintenance. Journal of Clinical Child Psychology. 2010;**27**:35-45. DOI: 10.1207/s15374424jccp2701_4

[30] Bagner DM, Eyberg SM. Parent-child interaction therapy for disruptive behavior in children with mental retardation: A randomized controlled trial. Journal of Clinical Child Adolescent Psychology. 2007;**36**:418-429. DOI: 10.1080/15374410701448448

[31] Bagner DM, Sheinkopf SJ, Vohr BR, Lester BM. Parenting intervention for externalizing behavior problems in children born premature: An initial examination. Journal of Developmental and Behavioral Pediatrics. 2010;**31**:209-216. DOI: 10.1097/DBP.0b013e3181d5a294

[32] Ginn NC, Clionsky LN, Eyberg SM, Warner-Metzger C, Abner JP. Child-directed interaction training for young children with autism spectrum disorders: Parent and child outcomes. Journal of Clinical Child and Adolescent Psychology. 2015;**46**:101-109. DOI: 10.1080/15374416.2015.1015135

[33] Lesack R, Bearss K, Celano M, Sharp WG. Parent–child interaction therapy and autism spectrum disorder: Adaptations with a child with severe developmental delays. Clinical Practice in Pediatric Psychlogy. 2014;**2**:68. DOI: 10.1037/cpp0000047

[34] Pincus DB, Eyberg SM, Cholate ML. Adapting parent–child interaction therapy for young children with separation anxiety disorder. Education and Treatment of Children. 2005;**28**:163-181

[35] Puliafico AC, Comer JS, Pincus DB. Adapting parent-child interaction therapy to treat anxiety disorders in young children. Child and Adolescent Psychiatric Clinics. 2012;**3**:607-619. DOI: 10.1016/j.chc.2012.05.005

[36] Carpenter AL, Puliafico AC, Kurtz SMS, Pincus DB, Comer JS. Extending parent-child interaction therapy for early internalizing problems: New advances for an overlooked population. Clinical Child and Family Psychology Review. 2014;**17**:340-356. DOI: 10.1007/s10567-014-0172-4

[37] Lenze SN, Pautsch J, Luby J. Parent-child interaction therapy emotion development: A novel treatment for depression in preschool children. Depression and Anxiety. 2010;**28**:153-159. DOI: 10.1002/da.20770

[38] Luby J, Lenze S, Tillman R. A novel early intervention for preschool depression: Findings from a pilot randomized controlled trial. Journal of Child Psychology and Psychiatry. 2012;**53**:313-322. DOI: 10.1111/j.1469-7610.2011.02483.x

[39] Timmer SG, Urquiza AJ, Zebell NM, McGrath JM. Parent-child interaction therapy: Application to maltreated parent-child dyads. Child Abuse and Neglect. 2005;**29**:825-842. DOI: 10.1016/j.chiabu.2005.01.003

[40] Thomas R, Zimmer-Gembeck MJ. Accumulating evidence for parent-child interaction therapy in the prevention of child maltreatment. Child Development. 2011;**82**:177-192. DOI: 10.1111/j.1467-8624.2010.01548.x

[41] Matos M, Bauermeister JJ, Bernal G. Parent-child interaction therapy for Puertorican preschool children with ADHD and behavioral problems: A pilot efficacy study. Family Process. 2009;**48**:232-252. DOI: 10.1111/j.1545-5300.2009.01279.x

[42] McCabe K, Yeh M. Parent-child interaction therapy for mexican americans: A randomized clinical trial. Journal of Clinical Child and Adolescent Psychology. 2009;**38**:753-759. DOI: 10.1080/15374410903103544

[43] McCabe KM, Yeh M, Garland AF, Lau AS, Chavez G. The GANA program: A tailoring approach to adapting parent child interaction therapy for mexican americans. Education and Treatment of Children. 2005;**28**:111-129

[44] BigFoot D, Funderburk BW. Honoring children, making relatives: The cultural translation of parent-child interaction therapy for american indian and Alaska native families. Journal of Psychoactive Drugs. 2011;**43**:309-318. DOI: 10.1080/02791072.2011.628924

[45] Leung C, Tsang S, Ng GSH, Choi SY. Efficacy of parent-child interaction therapy with Chinese ADHD children: Randomized controlled trial. Research on Social Work Practice. 2017;**27**:36-47. DOI: 10.1177/1049731516643837

[46] Bjørseth Å, Wichstrøm L. Effectiveness of parent-child interaction therapy (PCIT) in the treatment of young children's behavior problems. A randomized controlled study. PLoS One. 2016;**11**:e0159845. DOI: 10.1371/journal.pone.0159845

[47] Niec LN, Barnett M, Prewett M, Shanley J. Group parent-child interaction therapy: A randomized control trial for the treatment of conduct problems in young children. Journal of Consulting and Clinical Psychology. 2016;**84**:682-698. DOI: 10.1037/a0040218

[48] Niec LN, Hemme JM, Yopp JM, Brestan EV. Parent-child interaction therapy: The rewards and challenges of a group format. Cognitive and Behavioral Practice. 2005;**12**:113-125. DOI: 10.1016/S1077-7229(05)80046-X

[49] Foley K, McNeil CB, Norman M, Wallace NM. Effectiveness of group format parent-child interaction therapy compared to treatment as usual in a community outreach organization. Child & Family Behavior Therapy. 2016;**38**:279-298. DOI: 10.1080/07317107.2016.1238688

[50] Urquiza AJ, McNeil CB. Parent-child interaction therapy: An intensive dyadic intervention for physically abusive families. Child Maltreatment. 1996;**1**:134-144. DOI: 10.1177/1077559596001002005

[51] Graziano PA, Bagner DM, Slavec J, Hungerford G, Kent K, Babinski D, et al. Feasibility of intensive parent–child interaction therapy (I-PCIT): Results from an open trial. Journal of Psychopathology and Behavioral Assessment. 2014;**37**:38-49. DOI: 10.1007/s10862-014-9435-0

[52] Lyon AR, Gershenson RA, Farahmand FK, Thaxter PJ, Behling S, Budd KS. Effectiveness of teacher-child interaction training (TCIT) in a preschool setting. Behavior Modification. 2009;**33**:855-884. DOI: 10.1177/0145445509344215

[53] Budd KS, Baracz LL, Carter JS. Collaborating with public school partners to implement teacher-child interaction training (TCIT) as universal prevention. School Mental Health. 2015;**8**(2):207-221. DOI: 10.1007/s12310-015-9158-8

[54] Masse JJ, McNeil CB. In-home parent-child interaction therapy: Clinical considerations. Child and Family Behavior Therapy. 2008;**30**:127-135. DOI: 10.1080/07317100802060310

[55] Ware LM, McNeil CB, Masse J, Stevens S. Efficacy of in-home parent-child interaction therapy. Child and Family Behavior Therapy. 2008;**30**:99-126. DOI: 10.1080/07317100802060302

[56] Gresl BL, Fox RA, Fleischmann A. Home-based parent-child therapy in low-income African American, Caucasian, and Latino families: A

comparative examination of treatment outcomes. Child & Family Behavior Therapy. 2014;**36**:33-50. DOI: 10.1080/07317107.2014.878193

[57] Bagner DM, Garcia D, Hill R. Direct and indirect effects of behavioral parent training on infant language production. Behavior Therapy. 2016;**47**:184-197. DOI: 10.1016/j.beth.2015.11.001

[58] Bagner DM, Coxe S, Hungerford GM, Garcia D, Barroso NE, Hernandez J, et al. Behavioral parent training in infancy: A window of opportunity for high-risk families. Journal of Abnormal Child Psychology. 2016;**44**:901-912. DOI: 10.1007/s10802-015-0089-5

[59] Garcia D, Rodriquez GM, Hill RM, Lorenzo NE, Bagner DM. Infant language production and parenting skills: A randomized controlled trail. Behavior Therapy. 2018;**50**:544-557. DOI: 10.1016/j.beth.2018.09.003

[60] Morningstar M, Garcia D, Dirks MA, Bagner DM. Changes in parental prosody mediate effect of parent-training intervention on infant language production. Journal of Consulting and Clinical Psychology. 2019;**2019**(87):313-318. DOI: 10.1037/ccp0000375

[61] Carter AS, Briggs-Gowan MJ. Manual for the Infant Toddler Social & Emotional Assessment (ITSEA)—Version 2. San Antonio, Texas: Psychological Corporation, Harcourt Press; 2006

[62] Zimmerman IL, Steiner VG, Pond RA. The Preschool Language Scale-5. San Antonio, TX: Pearson; 2011

[63] Eyberg SM, Nelson MM, Ginn NC, Bhuiyan N, Boggs SR. Dyadic Parent-Child Interaction Coding System: Comprehensive Manual for Research and Training. 4th ed. Gainesville, FL: PCIT International; 2013

[64] Abidin RR. PSI-4 Professional Manual. Psychological Assessment Resources: Lutz, FL; 2012

[65] Radloff LS. The CES-D scale: A self-report depression scale for research in the general population. Applied Psychological Measurement. 1977;**1**. DOI: 10.1177/014662167700100306

Chapter 4

Where Technology Meets Psychology: Improving Global Mental Health

Martha Escobar Lux and Juan Manuel Escobar

Abstract

Mental health disorders are a growing concern worldwide. Unfortunately, they are not limited to a single demographic group, and there are not enough mental health professionals to evaluate every case. Training other healthcare providers in mental health topics is a possibility; nevertheless, relying on face-to-face training alone is not scalable. The use of technology has become an essential and feasible opportunity to address global education challenges. Furthermore, the use of e-learning could be an important strategy to reach effective mental health care and address disparities worldwide. This paper describes the importance of e-learning and e-MH (e-mental health) leaning for health providers and the possibility of e-learning as a solution to strengthen human resources for mental health globally. The use of e-MH learning creates an opportunity to overcome social, geographical, economic, and educational barriers and to train worldwide health professionals in mental health.

Keywords: e-learning, e-MH, technology-enabled learning, online learning, online education programs

1. Introduction

Mental health disparities are an urgent global issue, and we must take action. According to the United Nations, mental disorders are a leading cause of disability, accounting for 7.4% of disability-adjusted life years (DALYs) worldwide in 2010, a 38% increase since 1990 [1]. Furthermore, one in four people worldwide will suffer from depression, anxiety, or some other forms of mental illness over their lifetime [2]. Unfortunately, the situation is not better for children and adolescents, and the World Health Organization (WHO) has predicted that the burden of internalizing disorders in children and adolescents will surpass that of HIV by 2030 [3]. In Europe and the Americas, mental disorders among children aged 5-14 years ranked third among the causes of DALYs in 2000 and second in 2015 [4]. Most regions in the world had approximately 4 mental disorders in the top 20 diseases that cause the most DALYs in children aged 5–14 years. Conduct disorders and anxiety disorders were among the first two [4]. A meta-analysis published in 2015, including 27 countries and every region of the world, estimated a worldwide prevalence of mental disorders in children and adolescents of 13.4% [5].

Mental health is a pressing global health issue due to its burden, high prevalence, and alarming inequalities in access, stigma, treatment, and training. These factors are not just the result of low funding into the field of mental health. A lack of workforce and inadequate workforce training is another significant factor associated with the unequal burden of mental health globally [1]. The World Health Organization estimates that there is a shortage of about 7.2 million healthcare workers globally, and by 2035, this number will increase to 12.9 million [6]. Training health workers is one key initiative to improve this critical problem.

Global mental healthcare providers face several challenges, particularly in underserved and rural areas. These challenges include not only insufficient training but also a lack of physical resources, heavy caseloads, limited time, and the absence of referral services [7]. Training programs for psychiatrists are present in only 55% of low-income countries, 69% of low-middle-income countries, and 60% of upper-middle-income countries [8]. Gaps in delivering mental health training can be mitigated through continued training [8], which has proven to be one effective way to undertake challenges brought by disparities [7]. However, continued education is not easily accessible to many health providers due to time constraints, expenses, and geographic barriers [7].

With the advances in technology, online learning platforms have become more accessible in many fields, including health. Electronic learning or e-learning is defined as education delivered through an electronic form [9]. The term e-mental health or e-MH refers to mental health education, training, treatment, or screening through an electronically based approach.

2. e-Learning

e-Learning is defined as the use of "technology and services (e.g., computer or electronic device) to provide training or learning material including tutorials, simulations, case-based, and game-based, learning modules" [10]. e-Learning modalities include, but are not limited to, CD-ROMs, e-books, and Microsoft PowerPoint presentations to more complex virtual courses [9]. A helpful resource to understand the different levels of e-learning is with Alexander's four-level model of e-learning [11]. The first level is about online presentations and publishing, for example, review an article uploaded by a professor. The second level includes online quizzes and assessments. The third level comprises online forums in which participating students are provided with feedback and have the opportunity to engage in an online discussion. The fourth includes interactive learning through role-play, face-to-face exchanges, debates, etc. As the levels increase, e-learning becomes more similar to traditional face-to-face learning, and the trainer becomes more involved with the student's learning process.

Most e-learning courses require a trainer or instructor that is responsible for the content of the program. This person could be a professor at a university, a medical doctor at a hospital training program, etc. The trainer has different obligations depending on the level. For the first level, the trainer would be responsible for selecting readings for students, including the creation of any material such as PowerPoint presentations. In the second level, the trainer selects the information, creates evaluation systems, corrects them, and delivers feedback. For the more interactive third and fourth levels, the trainer will provide classes and lead other activities, just like a face-to-face model of training. Although trainers are not involved with the technological creation of the program, they are involved with the content and content delivery [11].

Initially, three main characteristics made e-learning different from the conventional face-to-face learning approach: asynchronicity (lack of unity of time), decentralization (lack of unity of place), and electronically mediated interaction and communication [12]. The lack of time and place create a different form of communication between the trainer and the student, with an absence of preverbal communication and more close contact [12]. As technology has improved and depending on the type of course, e-learning can also be synchronous, for example, when doing online debates in which every student needs to log in at a specific time with the trainer.

2.1 Advantages

e-Learning is a student-centered model that allows students to learn and study at their own pace and on their schedules [10]. Efforts are centered around learning and the student's needs, not the teachers' [12]. It is, therefore, an individualized model, based on innovative and interactive methods of education in an "information-rich environment" [12]. Additionally, materials must be accessible for students at all times, so that students can review them as many times as they need it. Having available materials also requires the teachers to have the content prepared before the start of the course, which ensures higher quality [12].

High-quality health education is limited in several regions of the world [13]. With the fast and ongoing advances in medicine, being up to date with the latest treatments and interventions can be impossible for the majority of health providers. Nevertheless, e-learning has become an attractive way to improve these limitations, given its affordability, flexibility (in time and location given its asynchronous and decentralized nature [12]), accessibility, and capacity-building potential in those places that need it the most [13, 14]. e-Learning is more affordable than traditional face-to-face learning since operational costs (physical classroom, accommodation, and travel) are lower.

2.2 Disadvantages

The personal interaction between trainers and students is considerably altered in e-learning, and some trainers fear that this will end up affecting the learning process [12]. For trainers, the preparation of e-learning courses is very different from face-to-face classes and requires a different skill set. For one thing, trainers need to develop competencies in technology and in teaching in virtual environments [12]. Since trainers may face a technology learning curve and also need to prepare in advance of the class sessions, e-learning demands more time from trainers than traditional face-to-face training sessions [12].

Although e-learning is more affordable than face-to-face courses and more flexible, it is still based on the assumption that the student has technology that is appropriate for the course. While e-learning has the opportunity to make education more universal, the need for technology is still an impediment to some parts of the population who want to engage with e-learning. Nonetheless, from 2000 to 2015, Internet access has increased by 806% [15]. The most significant increase in access has occurred in Africa [15].

Language can also be a limitation when benefiting from these courses since they are usually in English. Although translating courses can be expensive and complicated, its need often depends on the target's audience literacy and education level [16]. e-Learning can overcome some of these barriers, as long as the program is "sensitive to the level of availability of infrastructure, [and has] technical support, [a] clear policy on implementation, evaluation and curriculum re-orientation" [16].

2.3 Effectiveness

Although it is still a growing model, e-learning has been used to provide medical education and has proven to be equally effective as a face-to-face instructor-delivered training [17]. Several systemic reviews have concluded that the perceived experience of instructors and students is useful in the acquisition of clinical skills [12]. A program conducted in Kenya to support healthcare workers with respiratory infection control reported that the knowledge gains were almost equal between face-to-face and e-learning groups [16]. However, e-learning research has primarily focused on student's satisfaction and knowledge improvement, and it still needs to evaluate behavioral changes in healthcare professionals [9].

3. e-Mental health (e-MH) learning

e-Mental health is the use of technological tools and media to "provide screening, health promotion, prevention, early intervention, treatment, or relapse prevention as well as for improvement of health care delivery (e.g. electronic patient files), professional education (e-learning), and online research in the field of mental health" [18].

Given the global need to improve mental care, e-MH is one of the fastest-growing fields. e-MH is mainly for treatment programs and monitoring systems. With the use of apps, email, and the Internet, monitoring systems have been created as a supplement from clinical consultation for patients [15]. For example, the True Colors self-management system is an app created by Oxford University to help patients with bipolar disorders to monitor their symptoms and plan activities better [15]. Another e-MH has been web-based treatment programs such as electronic psychotherapy interventions, telepsychiatry (TP), or telemental health (TMH) [19], for patients suffering from depression, anxiety, eating disorders, substance abuse, and dependence [20]. Although there are many types of psychotherapies, most of these online interventions are based on the cognitive behavioral therapy (CBT) model, since it is useful and relatively simple to use through electronic media. In CBT, mental health providers act as trainers that teach patients several skills to better recognize symptoms and techniques to address them [18]. CBT has been effective in various mental disorders and has a structure that makes it compatible with technological platforms.

e-MH has not been utilized as much in professional education (e-learning), but it is becoming a pressing need given the shortage of healthcare providers and the increasing demands in mental health. While the availability of online programs that provide psychotherapy teaching to mental health providers is limited, existing research does indicate comparable efficacy results between e-learning and face-to-face mental health training [14]. The Queensland Centre for Mental Health Learning offers different online education options for mental health professionals. Recently, their sensory modulation approach program was tested on 121 participants, with positive results in improved knowledge and acceptability [14].

So far, positive results have been found in the use of e-MH for patients through educational apps, monitoring programs, and telepsychiatry. Now the challenge is to use e-MH as teaching platforms for mental health providers. Given the simplicity of cognitive behavioral therapy and its easy incorporation into electronic modules, CBT may be one of the first e-learning options for mental health personnel.

3.1 e-MH for children's mental health

According to the American Academy of Child and Adolescent Psychiatry (AACAP), there are approximately 8300 practicing child psychiatrists in the United States and more than 15 million children and adolescents with a particular need that requires the expertise of a child and adolescent psychiatrist [21]. This situation invariably leads to a delay in treatment or even no treatment at all [21].

Unfortunately, this disproportion might seem better than that of other countries, where the number of child psychiatrists is even lower. Furthermore, children and adolescents living in poverty conditions have a higher risk for mental disorders but are less likely to receive the appropriate help [22]. It is prevalent for people with mental disorders or difficulties to never see an expert; therefore, primary care providers are an essential solution in addressing mental health concerns [22]. With this in mind and the importance of promoting mental health in children and adolescents, e-MH has also become a solution in this area.

The Resource for Advancing Children's Health (REACH) institute is a nonprofit organization committed to ensuring up-to-date mental healthcare reaches everyone who needs it, through innovative training to primary care providers. Participants initially attend a 3-day interactive course in diagnosis and treatment of various mental health topics, followed by a 6-month case-based e-learning system. This program has consistently and successfully trained hundreds and extended throughout the United States and other countries. Other programs, such as the ECHO project, use video conference technology to train primary care clinicians in mental health, HIV, chronic pain, and endocrinology, among others. The mental health initiative in Cincinnati offers clinicians online support to improve the treatment and monitoring of their patients.

4. Considerations when creating a successful e-MH learning program

Self-paced modules, interactive activities, case scenarios, opportunities for self-reflection, and links to further information and resources are convenient when creating online learning platforms [14]. Also, the option to reassess the lessons following the completion of the training allows students to review the material and make the most out of it [14].

Learning strategies rooted in theory serve as a useful foundation when designing an e-MH learning program. For example, the Train-the-Trainer model is based on the Adult Learning Theory, which implies that learning works best when peers provide its resources. Also, the diffusion of innovation theory suggests that people adopt information better when it is provided by a social network they trust [23]. Some e-learning websites only provide digitalized versions of textbooks or courses, making the learner's experience more like reading an "electronic book" instead of being part of a class [10]. The social-cultural learning theory suggests the increased use of situated learning, which provides learners with representations of real-life experiences to solve and reflect on [10]. Situated e-learning "is defined as a computer-assisted educational program constructed with simulated situations, scenarios-based, or case-based learning activities" [10]. For example, the creation of virtual patients with a specific set of symptoms, lab tests, clinical course, and questions mimics the real-world and encourages the learner to acquire skills and knowledge to manage and solve unique situations [10]. Situated learning is an effective method to improve clinical students' knowledge and abilities while avoiding unnecessary risks of real patient encounters [10].

5. Organizational barriers and solutions to e-learning

The many advantages of e-learning have also presented the opportunity to study and better understand its limitations. The HeXL project (Health eXL: Surmounting the barriers to NHS e-learning in the North-East) is one of the many projects that aim to identify the obstacles and limitations of e-learning in NHS staff and healthcare students, to overcome them [24].

5.1 Organizational barriers

The HeXL project identified the following organizational barriers: adopting and developing e-learning programs is time-consuming, quality standards are lacking, modules need to be carefully scheduled, and marketing can be problematic [24]. Another considerable concern includes change management. Some trainers may have concerns about the process of change, lack the required skills to develop and teach an e-learning program, and lack time to do so, since developing an e-learning program is more time-consuming for trainers than traditional face-to-face approaches [24].

At the managerial level, solutions are related to the commitment of both institutions and trainers, the cooperation between departments, and the inclusion of software providers and trainers. Culture shift strategies, as well as planning and implementation processes with appropriate resource management, are key strategies to overcome organizational barriers [24]. As for the trainers, it is crucial to have a good collaboration between content, pedagogy, and technology. Trainers also need time to master the technique and to adapt their teaching styles to online sessions.

5.2 Economic barriers

e-Learning has some additional costs compared to the traditional learning scenario, which can be divided into initial fixed costs including hardware cost, start-up costs, equipment, and training and ongoing variable costs such as software, licenses, keeping equipment up-to-date, program development, and training, among others [24]. In this case, it is vital to know the real costs of the program, including its cost-effectiveness and cost-benefit analysis. For students, e-learning costs are usually low or even free, since operational expenses (travel and accommodation) are reduced compared to traditional learning [11]. Some programs, such as the Global Health eLearning Center, offer free courses. Nevertheless, this initiative is not always incentivized, since there is some discussion surrounding how payment makes students more involved with the program [24]. Course costs could be adapted to the income of the country, or, if the courses are associated with an institution involved in research, charges could be reduced if participants agree to participate in survey studies.

5.3 Hardware and software barriers

Technology is an especially challenging barrier since not enough research and innovation have been done in e-learning programs. Both trainers and learners need to feel comfortable with the program and have easy access to it [11]. The hardware must be reliable, and problems need immediate solutions [24]. An excellent way to provide the best software is through the initial evaluation research on software packages, carefully designed software from the learner's and trainer's point of view, and a pilot test with feedback and following modifications [24].

5.4 Pedagogical barriers

There are various skepticisms around e-learning. Many have to do with the idea that traditional methods are better, that technology cannot be trusted, that there is no personal contact, and that the quality of education is not the same. While many of these problems are real, growing technological advances have surpassed many of these limitations [24]. However, the rejection of trainers toward e-learning also has to do with their fears about how to teach in an electronic setting. The competences of face-to-face teaching and e-learning are not the same, and with the increase of e-learning, a documented need for e-pedagogy is also rising [12].

To overcome these barriers, standards of quality need to be created as an integrated system between content, pedagogy, and technology. Courses need pilot tests and should be evaluated regularly [24]. Also, programs need to be tailored according to the needs of the trainers and learners. Although there is still not enough evidence to fully understand the roles and best teaching methods for educators [12], the involvement of educators in the creation of the program and the use of pilot tests and training on the software are good ways to help with the adoption process.

5.5 Adherence to e-learning programs

e-Learning poses a challenge when it comes to maintaining students' interest. Not having a face-to-face approach and relying more on self-paced learning pose a higher risk, since students' lack of engagement can lead to losing them as the course advances.

Since e-learning is a new educational system that comprehends a different way to relate to the instructor compared to the face-to-face approach, with a greater emphasis on individualized education and self-paced learning, maintaining a student's interest can be difficult. e-Learning might have a higher risk of not engaging students enough and therefore, losing them as the course advances.

To prevent attendance attrition, courses could include pre- and posttest quizzes and a final exam that test the student's knowledge and grant a certificate with a score higher to a certain percentage on the final exam [16]. Additionally, although it is easier to make the course asynchronous, synchronicity improves the student's learning experience as well as involvement with the course.

6. Looking ahead on e-MH learning

6.1 Task shifting

Task shifting is defined as "delegating tasks to existing or new cadres with either less training or narrowly tailored training" [8]. It is proven as an effective and feasible intervention in response to the shortage of mental health providers [8]. Although e-MH is being used mostly with physicians, the training can be extended to nonmedical mental health workers as another potential solution to improve mental healthcare disparities [7]. Although these health providers are not trained or licensed to diagnose and prescribe medication, they can be trained in psychotherapeutic techniques, which are known as task shifting [7].

Mental health e-learning can even be used for the general population, not only for patients to understand and track their diseases better but also for the general population to provide a mental health service when needed. In Australia, a Mental Health First Aid (MHFA) training course was developed for the general population to improve mental health first aid skills [17]. There is an increasing prevalence in mental health disorders and in the number of natural and human-made disasters (terrorist attacks, earthquakes, tsunamis, etc.), which can trigger existing mental illnesses or cause psychological symptoms. As a result, having the general population trained on mental health first aid is an essential first response, while appropriate professional help is received or crises are resolved.

6.2 Increasing enrollment

e-MH learning also works as an innovative way to improve mental health education for medical students. Not all medical students have access to psychiatrists and psychologists that can teach them. Others, on the contrary, do but not always feel comfortable with the subject of mental illness. Patients with mental illness often cause fear in medical students. Additionally, negative attitudes from medical students toward psychiatry are explained by the perception that psychiatry is not scientific and not enjoyable and it does not include medical training in its practice [25]. The use of innovative educational initiatives increases knowledge about mental health, improves attitudes, and reduces stigma [25]. One example of this is the King's THET Somaliland Partnership (KTSP), which works to strengthen health care through the exchange of knowledge, skills, and experience between Somaliland and King's Health Partners in the United Kingdom [25]. To improve attitudes toward psychiatry, the KTSP mental health group provided teaching to medical students in Somaliland, who did not have any previous training in psychiatry. By the end of the course, there was a positive association between this brief education process and positive attitudes toward psychiatry [25].

The amount of mental health workers is limited, and, in part, this is related to medical students' negative attitudes toward psychiatry and mentally ill patients, which translates into a reduction of recruitment into psychiatry. e-MH learning could improve medical students' attitudes toward mental health and, therefore, increase enrollment in psychiatry residency programs.

7. Conclusion

The increasing prevalence of mental disorders has become an alarming problem, especially in children and adolescents. Its negative consequences extend from the patient to his/her family, community, health system, and society. Furthermore, there are critical inequities in mental health that make it even more challenging to address. Global mental health inequities are manifested in different ways. Some are related to insufficient access and therapies, others with limited promotion and prevention campaigns, and others with scarcity in mental health workforce and training.

The discussion about the workforce has become imperative, as the world leaders are trying to achieve more comprehensive and universal health coverages. Dr. Carissa Etienne, WHO Regional Director for the Americas, mentions that one of the challenges for reaching global health coverage is "ensuring that everyone—especially people in vulnerable communities and remote areas—has access to well-trained, culturally-sensitive and competent health staff" [6]. An analysis of the global workforce by the Joint Learning Initiative highlighted the need to strengthen human resources for health through the creation of knowledge and continuous learning opportunities [16]. e-Learning is becoming a necessary intervention to address global education challenges. Research regarding the use of health learning platforms has been effective. With growing evidence to support its use, the need to train health providers in mental health topics should be the next step.

Where Technology Meets Psychology: Improving Global Mental Health
DOI: http://dx.doi.org/10.5772/intechopen.88174

Author details

Martha Escobar Lux[1*] and Juan Manuel Escobar[2,3]

1 The REACH Institute, New York, NY, USA

2 Hospital Universitario Fundación Santa Fe de Bogotá, Colombia

3 Universidad de los Andes – Facultad de Medicina, Bogotá, Colombia

*Address all correspondence to: martha@thereachinstitute.org

IntechOpen

© 2019 The Author(s). Licensee IntechOpen. This chapter is distributed under the terms of the Creative Commons Attribution License (http://creativecommons.org/licenses/by/3.0), which permits unrestricted use, distribution, and reproduction in any medium, provided the original work is properly cited.

References

[1] Farrington C, Aristidou A, Ruggeri K. mHealth and global mental health: Still waiting for the mH 2 wedding? Globalization and Health. 2014;**10**(17):1-8. Available from: http://www.globalizationandhealth.com/content/10/1/17

[2] Pike K. Want a Safer, More Prosperous World? Invest in Mental Health. 18 August 2015. Retrieved from: https://thehill.com/blogs/congress-blog/healthcare/251312-want-a-safer-more-prosperous-world-invest-in-mental-health

[3] Kato N, Yanagawa T, Fujiwara T, Morawska A. Prevalence of children's mental health problems and the effectiveness of population-level family interventions. Journal of Epidemiology. 2015;**25**(8):507-516

[4] Baranne ML, Falissard B. Global burden of mental disorders among children aged 5-14 years. Child and Adolescent Psychiatry and Mental Health. 2018;**12**(1):1-9

[5] Polanczyk GV, Salum GA, Sugaya LS, Caye A, Rohde LA. Annual research review: A meta-analysis of the worldwide prevalence of mental disorders in children and adolescents. The Journal of Child Psychology and Psychiatry and Allied Disciplines. 2015;**56**(3):345-365

[6] World Health Organization. Global health workforce shortage to reach 12.9 million in coming decades [Internet]. 2013. Available from: http://www.who.int/mediacentre/news/releases/2013/health-workforce-shortage/en/

[7] Ravitz P, Cooke RG, Mitchell S, Reeves S, Teshima J, Lokuge B, et al. Continuing education to go: Capacity building in psychotherapies for front-line mental health workers in underserviced communities. Canadian Journal of Psychiatry. 2013;**58**(6):335-343

[8] Kakuma R, Minas H, van Ginneken N, Dal Poz MR, Desiraju K, Morris JE, et al. Global mental health 5 human resources for mental health care: Current situation and strategies for action. Lancet. 2011;**378**(9803):1654-1663

[9] Sinclair PM, Kable A, Levett-Jones T, Booth D. The effectiveness of Internet-based e-learning on clinician behaviour and patient outcomes: A systematic review. International Journal of Nursing Studies. 2016;**57**:70-81

[10] Feng J-Y, Chang Y-T, Chang H-Y, Erdley WS, Lin C-H, Chang Y-J. Systematic review of effectiveness of situated E-learning on medical and nursing education. Worldviews on Evidence-Based Nursing. 2013;**10**(3):174-183. DOI: 10.1111/wvn.12005

[11] Chang V. International journal of information management review and discussion: E-learning for academia and industry. International Journal of Information Management. 2016;**36**(3):476-485. DOI: 10.1016/j.ijinfomgt.2015.12.007

[12] Koch LF. The nursing educator's role in e-learning: A literature review. Nurse Education Today. 2014;**34**(11):1382-1387. DOI: 10.1016/j.nedt.2014.04.002

[13] Murphy R, Clissold E, Keynejad RC. Problem-based, peer-to-peer global mental health e-learning between the UK and Somaliland: A pilot study. Evidence-Based Mental Health. 2017;**20**(4):140-144

[14] Meredith P, Yeates H, Greaves A, Taylor M, Slattery M, Charters M, et al. Preparing mental health professionals for new directions in mental health practice: Evaluating the sensory approaches e-learning training package. International Journal of Mental Health Nursing. 2018;**27**(1):106-115

[15] Smith KA, Tomlin A, Cipriani A, Geddes JR. Evidence-based mental health and e-learning: A guide for clinicians. BJPsych Advances. 2016;**22**(1):55-63. DOI: 10.1192/apt.bp.113.012377

[16] Mwaikambo L, Avila M, Mazursky S, Nallathambi K. Utilizing eLearning to strengthen the capacity of global health practitioners and institutions around the world. Knowledge Management & E-Learning. 2012;**4**(3):293-309

[17] Jorm AF, Kitch-Ener BA, Fischer J-A, Cvetkovski S, Fellow R, Kitchener BA. Mental health first aid training by e-learning: A randomized controlled trial. The Australian and New Zealand Journal of Psychiatry. 2010;**44**:1072-1081

[18] Musiat P, Tarrier N. Collateral outcomes in e-mental health: A systematic review of the evidence for added benefits of computerized cognitive behavior therapy interventions for mental health. Psychological Medicine. 2014;**44**(15):3137-3150

[19] Hilty DM, Crawford A, Teshima J, Chan S, Sunderji N, Yellowlees PM, et al. A framework for telepsychiatric training and e-health: Competency-based education, evaluation and implications. International Review of Psychiatry. 2015;**27**(6):569-592

[20] Andersson G, Titov N. Advantages and limitations of internet based interventions for common mental disorders. World Psychiatry. 2014;**13**(2):4-11. DOI: 10.1002/wps.20083

[21] AACAP. Workforce Issues [Internet]. 2019. Available from: https://www.aacap.org/aacap/resources_for_primary_care/workforce_issues.aspx

[22] Hodgkinson S, Godoy L, Beers LS, Lewin A. Improving mental health access for low-income children and families in the primary care setting. Pediatrics. 2016;**139**(1):e20151175

[23] De Beurs DP, De Groot MH, De Keijser J, Mokkenstorm J, Van Duijn E, De Winter RFP, et al. The effect of an e-learning supported train-the-trainer programme on implementation of suicide guidelines in mental health care. Journal of Affective Disorders. 2015;**175**:446-453

[24] Childs S, Blenkinsopp E, Hall A, Walton G. Effective e-learning for health professionals and students-barriers and their solutions. A systematic review of the literature-findings from the HeXL project. Health Information and Libraries Journal. 2005;**22**(s2):20-32. DOI: 10.1111/j.1470-3327.2005.00614.x

[25] Keynejad R, Garratt E, Adem G, Finlayson A, Whitwell S, Sheriff RS. Improved attitudes to psychiatry: A global mental health peer-to-peer E-learning partnership. Academic Psychiatry. 2016;**40**(4):659-666

Chapter 5

Pregnancy in Adolescence: A Hallmark of Forthcoming Perinatal Depression?

Alexandra Matei and Cringu Antoniu Ionescu

Abstract

Over the last decades, teenage sexual behavior has come to expand toward unknown grounds mostly under the constant change in sociopolitical and cultural background. Whether they culminate in unintended pregnancies or not, adolescent reproductive health issues reside basically in the lack of proper implementation of educational programs and/or difficulty in accessing contraceptive methods. Until now, retrospective studies succeeded to identify a few characteristics correlated with adolescent pregnancies and their outcomes, while in low-income countries, socioeconomical disadvantages play a significant role in the lives of pregnant teenagers, and mental health affections such as depression and anxiety as well as noxious behavior are typically the appanage of high-income countries. By establishing cultural- and geographical-related peculiarities of young patients with impact on their pregnancy, raising awareness toward the spread of this new trend in obstetrical medicine might prove to be effective in practice when counseling these patients.

Keywords: teenage pregnancy, depression, unintended pregnancy, sexual education, fetal outcome

1. Introduction

Transition from childhood to adult life is known to be an experience engaging infinite possibilities with unpredictable outcomes. Adolescence or the time period between 10 and 19 years of age represents the nucleus of personal development from the primary inherited self toward building a complex self-identity. The response of individuals exposed to endless possibilities arising from surrounding events and phenomena is what builds up one's character and nature. Because of the absence of experience along with emotional immaturity—both contributing to a circle of weaknesses—it is considered that teenagers embody a vulnerable population. Therefore, investing in worldwide efforts destined to assure good healthcare for this specific part of the population is well justified.

Nowadays, the UNICEF states that 16% of the world population (1.2 billion people) is adolescents [1]. The youth's morbidity emerges from mental health issues, depressive disorders, anxiety, and behavioral problems, which are known to affect adolescent well-being [2]. Social norms have a different impact on young people, especially depending on gender. Specifically, female teenagers have increased mortality and morbidity rates directly related to pregnancy in early stages of transition to adulthood; reports show that approximately 12 million girls aged 15–19 years and at least 777,000 girls under 15 years give birth each year in developing regions, and at the same time, unintended pregnancies affect almost 10 million girls aged 15–19 years old [3]. These concerning statistics and the subsidiary connections between pregnancy body transformation and adolescent psychological immature integrity raised awareness toward this cluster of issues and formed the basis for the sustainable development goal 3 addressed by the United Nations. Preliminary data published in 2019 show that adolescent fertility declined from 56 births per 1000 adolescent women in 2000 to 44 births in 2019; this is promising information regarding the target set to ensure universal access to sexual and reproductive healthcare services until 2030 [4].

It might come as a paradox the fact that in the era of globalization and ultramodern communication devices, teenage access to health guidance and education is still facing serious obstacles [1]. International organizations are starting to use tools as Google Trends in order to identify and respond to the unmet need for proper networking and health services. Moreover, an emerging area of interest called "infodemiology" has been implemented by Eysenbach after epidemiologists came to the conclusion that health-related information seeking affects each individual's demands for healthcare services and increases healthcare utilization [5, 6]. Assessing data in real time has become crucial under most aspects of our lives, but nevertheless, there are still low- and middle-income countries where information on an inhabitant's health status is not available. For example, evaluations for mental disorders in people aged 5–17 years are available for only 6–7% of countries reviewed in the Global Burden of Disease project, while suicide remains the second-highest cause of death among people aged 15 to 29 globally [2, 4].

2. Divergent societies: one common problem

Over the last decades, significant attention has been drawn toward adolescent health, especially since severe social and economic consequences are involved in this matter. In several societies depending on cultural values, pregnancy in young women is considered a vector of poverty transmission from one generation to another [7]. Tendency toward school dropout, reduced employment rates, and engagement in noxious behaviors are all social issues related to adolescent pregnancy [7, 8]. Furthermore, the severe impact of all the aforementioned factors on mental health integrity under the shape of stigma or rejection are all leading causes of increased associated morbidity [8]. Articles addressing a global perspective on teenage pregnancy acknowledged the role of the family structure, whether intact or dysfunctional, on young people's sexual behavior: it has been shown that a close relationship between parents and teenagers based on communication and support has an actual impact on diminishing teenage high-risk behaviors [8].

In the attempt to draw the limits of this international concern, populational studies have estimated that the proportion of adolescent population reached a peak around 1980, from then on being predicted with a decreasing tendency until 2050; at that point, a new prominent increase is foreseen [7]. This demographic representation is, however, subject to change taking into account the alarming fluctuations in traveling populations and pandemics affecting health and life expectancy.

However, literature proves that adolescents engage in age-related risk behaviors irrespective of cultural and sociopolitical backgrounds: in Latin America and the Caribbean, adolescents play a significant role in the society since they account for almost 30% of the population; this way, it is relevant to mention a 2012 Mexican report that identified that 23% of 12–19-year-old adolescents already initiated their sexual life; however, 14.7% of the boys and 33.4% of the girls did not use contraceptive measures, and this conclusion had determined authorities to apply preventive strategies on this matter [7].

While most countries around the world struggle with reducing pregnancy and birth rates in adolescent populations, the United States of America managed to achieve a general decline in the rates mentioned above: in 2016 the birth rate of youths aged 15–19 years reached a historic low of 20.3 births per 1000 adolescents [9]; however, there are conflicting results regarding some vulnerable groups, including those teenagers who are homeless or incarcerated and those from rural areas or from small ethnic communities [10]. Here, adapting interventions and precision-focused strategies are still to be developed. In the attempt of breaking this harmful habit cycle, the United States have committed to invest more than 200 million dollars each year in abstinence programs [8]. By using a new perspective on an old problem, multiple interventions developed under legal criteria are destined to empower youths by helping them improve their decision-making abilities as well as preparing them for adulthood [9].

There are studies that describe teenage pregnancy as a positive experience as well [11]; the adolescent perspective on the matter is the main indicator in this theory. Themes from the literature include the search for autonomy, peer recognition, and a place in society. In this research pregnancy is marked as a life project to provide the unfulfilled needs of youngsters. Most of the time, young women who assume motherhood are still operating at different levels—emotional, financial, and cognitive—dependent on other persons; however, there are widespread small communities that are known to recognize early marriage as a tradition, bound by religious and not civil rules.

It is, therefore, a demanding challenge to solve the teenage birth problem using a single solution. Distinctive nations require distinctive measures which fit more or less depending on the surrounding macroenvironment. Taking a step back and learning from the past could help notice that over time the rates in adolescent fertility have remained high in sub-Saharan Africa at around 101 births per 1000 adolescent women [4]. At the opposite side is France with the lowest rates, marking 7 pregnancies per 1000 teenagers aged 15–19 years [11]. The pursuit of the etiology can sometimes reveal a potential connection between geographic area of residence, climate, and health issues. Nevertheless, a closer look on the cultural background of the teenage pregnancy debate is considered more appropriate in this chapter.

In 2013 15.6% of first children in Romania were born to teenage mothers, this being the highest proportion in the European Union according to Eurostat [12]. A social investigation carried in 2017 in this state showed that 6 out of 10 underage mothers never had access to sexual education and reproduction health counseling [13]. The magnitude of teenage pregnancy concern has been more allegiantly expressed by statistics in 2018 when data demonstrated that with respect to women under 19 years old, 12,906 were at their first birth, 3657 at their second, 673 at their third, 63 at their forth, 7 at their fifth, and 1 at her sixth birth [14]. The current situation in this Eastern European country might result from the direct consequences of its political history, i.e., the change from communist ideology into a democracy manifesto has left traces inside the community nucleus. Years before 1989, knowledge on teenage pregnancies was scarce, but the hardship of women with unintended pregnancies who lived under Decree 770, which outlawed abortion for women under 40 with fewer than four children, went beyond imagination. When fertility became an instrument of state control, a woman's right to decide what is best for her was no longer an option. As well as in other former Soviet countries, statistics in Romania are incomplete, but an increase in adolescent pregnancy has come to be known during the mid-1990s, and since then it reached the limits of a public health issue [1].

Cambodia, home to the largest adolescent and young adult population in the Southeast Asian region [15], went also through some major political changes during recent decades. The health infrastructure suffered severe damage after the genocide in 1970, and its recovery had been extremely difficult since then. Women in this region confront themselves with limited autonomy, low literacy, and poor wealth status. Consequently, unintended pregnancies mark a universal issue in this country even nowadays as Rizvi et al. concluded in their study following the use of Bronfenbrenner's social ecological model. This model was the theoretical basis for identifying factors influencing unintended pregnancies. It was in 2008 that Cambodia adopted a formal adolescent reproductive health policy, and later in 2016, the first sexual reproductive health literacy program was launched [15].

3. Selected pregnancy-related aspects linked to perinatal depression

When observing adolescents in their environment, it is important to notice the fact that experiences are what characterize people the most and not their values and beliefs [1]. Beyond religion, faith, and general convictions, personal response to events surrounding oneself is what builds characters and shape personalities [1]. As mentioned above, the sensitive topic of teenage pregnancy in some perceptions has a positive side as well even if there is still an existing global health issue.

Factors that were described by Rizvi et al. as predisposing to unintended pregnancies could as well take part in the outbreak of teenage pregnancy, whether they are related to the microenvironment, in the interpersonal, institutional, and community levels, including partners and peers, or to the macroenvironment, in the policy or relevant legislation level [15].

A different picture of "young motherhood" is described by Bas et al. in a study performed in Turkey: beside a lower prevalence of adolescent pregnancies compared to World Health Organization global data, 7.9% (3.5–12%) versus 11%, there was a higher likelihood of pregnancies in late adolescent years (18–19 years); plus, the majority of women were married, and pregnancies were desired in the study population. The authors also reported early marriage as a common practice in Turkey. At the same time, the study concluded that there was a specific need for adolescent mothers to prolong hospitalization stays in order to assure proper care and nutrition support for the newborn; 25.3% of the study group subjects were readmitted in the hospital 1 month postpartum due to infant inadequate weight in 34.4% of the cases [16].

An unfavorable fetal outcome following a teenage pregnancy—whether related to preterm delivery with low birth weight or a low Apgar score at 5 minutes or to a possible stillbirth—could provide stressful situations for any woman, especially an adolescent. Literature presents controversial information regarding adverse birth outcomes, and some studies conclude that once results are adjusted for other factors correlated with adverse birth events, early motherhood is not correlated with poorer neonatal status [17].

A large cohort study performed between 2009 and 2014 in Canada on 25,263 women concluded that teenage mothers had higher rates of depression during pregnancy (9.8%) compared to mothers aged 20–34 years (5.8%) and ≥ 35 years (6.8%) ($p < 0.001$) [17]. A possible explanation of these results might reside in the fact that more than 70% of adolescent pregnancies in Canada are unintended. How is it then, possible, that even in high-income countries where access to all kinds of informational materials is freely available that teenagers still engage in disruptive practices? The response to this question seems to be more complex than it looks.

On the matter of teenage mental health, the clash between civilizations is eloquent and understanding of what people grew up to value as their cultural legacy can prove to be an enriching and enlightening experience in the search of socially distinguishable factors involved in human behaviors.

The repercussions of an active reproductive teenage life on the psychological level usually manifests before giving birth, when women experience blame, critics, and social exclusion [7]. After delivery, motherhood responsibilities that sometimes are not shared by male partners can provide feelings of overwhelm, fear, anxiety, guilt, and shame [7]. In time, teenagers get to experiment depressive disorders originating in feelings of failure due to reduced employment opportunities and an inability to reintegrate in the social activities from before or due to denial of current situation [7, 8]. This is consistent with a study performed by Sanchez et al. where 41.7% of pregnant teenagers had emotional alterations due to financial factors, while in 7.8% of the study group, problems related to partners and family support were the main identified stressors [18].

Giving birth in adolescence implies peculiar events strictly dependable on the ability of the growing body to support the mechanism of labor. While in some states cesarean section is a compulsory medical management of birth in adolescents, studies performed in other countries recorded high rates of cephalopelvic disproportion (18.5%) or prolonged labor (16%) leading to emergency cesarean section delivery [7, 16]. Adding the increasing trend in practicing defensive medicine especially defensive cesarean sections, it comes as no surprise the report coming from a tertiary care unit from Bucharest revealing 71.6% rate of cesarean section in the adolescent study population [19].

4. Mind over matter is the goal but how do we get there?

In the search of best methods to be used in order to reduce the psychological vulnerabilities of teenagers, screening interventions play a significant role [19]. Nevertheless, therapeutic management is compulsory for every diagnosed patient.

Across the globe, Thailand has the highest rate of adolescent births in Southeast Asia and second-highest in the world [20]. It was the appropriate context to certify the usefulness of a questionnaire-based strategy implemented by a John Hopkins work team in order to assess birth preparedness and complication readiness (BPCR) in young mothers. Results obtained were encouraging, showing that a good BPCR score was present in 78.4% of cases, and further correlated mostly with pregnant women undergoing ≥ 4 antenatal consultations (odds ratio 3.2, 95% CI 1.13–9.05, p = 0.023) [20]. In other words, it is reassuring to find that with correct prenatal monitoring, not only good perinatal obstetrical and neonatal outcomes can be foreseen but also prevention of psychological disturbances can be achieved as well.

One of the best organized healthcare systems around the world is certainly the one from Sweden [21]. Oddly, this state has the highest abortion rate in Western Europe, while 23% of parous women never used any contraception method [21]. New patient-centered instruments were rapidly assessed in order to be implemented in primary care, and since nowadays 5% of all Internet searches are health-related, researchers considered that a reproductive life planning tool using a website could best benefit patients. Follow-up conclusions showed this strategy to be positively received by midwifes who in this country are licensed to prescribe contraceptives [21] and are in the frontline of promoting medical care. Accepting and exploring online networking as a supportive engine to promote healthy habits and access to medical guidance can actually make a difference. This is important especially in developed countries where education and access to information are no longer restricted areas of lifestyle.

Resuming the facts on perinatal depression, it is safe to say that patients suffering from this medical condition would best benefit from a multidisciplinary approach at the time of delivery or even earlier [21]. Birth-related psychological changes and further psychiatric ramifications represent a less explored field by obstetrician and midwives; this could explain why in many areas around the globe physicians tend to underestimate or even fail to recognize signs and symptoms leading to proper early diagnosis. Repercussions gravitate not only around the mother but also around the well-being of the fetus and of the entire family. Involvement of mothers of young age transforms this subject into a more confounding one.

Although information on the subject is still scarce, there are two recent trials presenting relevant and promising insights. The first one [22] was based on the screening for perinatal depression; a number of 8580 adults and 772 adolescents were assessed during pregnancy and 6 months after birth. Results showed that the incidence of depression in the teenage group was almost three times higher than the one in the adult group (17.7 and 6.9%, $p < 0.001$). Furthermore, despite the fact that there were no observed differences between the severity of depression, examination of patients diagnosed with perinatal depression revealed that adolescents had significantly different attitudes to pregnancy, motherhood, and parenting skills than adults. This trial draws equal conclusions with other similar assessments that support the body of evidence that younger maternal age is a strong predictor of adverse pregnancy outcomes [22]. This fact is also suggested by the outcome following remission of depression symptoms in the study groups: no improvement on parenting skills or motherhood adjustment was noted.

The second trial [23] is an ongoing cluster randomized trial based on a hybrid "effectiveness-implementation" plan specifically destined to assess a particular intervention package designed for teenagers with perinatal depression. The objectives of this study are directed toward improving maternal depression symptoms, and by achieving that, enhancing parental skills at 6 months postpartum assessment is also anticipated. Postnatal follow-up on the subjects is expected to end August 2020, and the results will be of interest given that it is considered to be the first trial to address the particular and unique needs of depressive pregnant adolescents.

Adhering to noxious behavior related to smoking, alcohol, and drug consumption, later favoring uncontrolled sexual practices culminating in unintended pregnancies can point out the preamble of depressive or anxiety disorders in adolescents [8]. Further interruption of education with associated guilt, absence of family support, and social rejection all contribute to predispose teenagers to misconduct [7].

There is strong evidence that girls are at a higher risk of developing depressive symptoms than their male counterparts, possible explanations being drawn after investigation of cognitive vulnerability deduced from negative ruminating style and negative cognitions [24]. There are also pregnancy and birth related events like premature delivery or giving birth to a low birth weight baby requiring additional neonatal support, which once added to the moment and mode of delivery itself – vaginal or by cesarean section – provide disturbances that may affect the psychic in a negative manner.

Facing unpredictable life situations like maternity sometimes interferes with other preexistent teenager struggles like body image concerns and eating or learning disorders [24].

Screening tools for early detection of depression have long been studied and improved, but it is a reality that beside being laborious, most of them can only be applied in practice by properly trained medical personnel—in truth, by psychologists and/or psychiatrists. In spite of efforts made to raise awareness on the subject of perinatal adolescent depression during the last decade, interestingly, only half of depressive adolescents are diagnosed before reaching adulthood [25], and this reality undeniably requires for clinical monitoring on any minor clinical sign of mood change.

On the general topic of child and teenage major depressive condition, numerous studies and interventional trials have been conducted. Comprehensive modern strategies integrate psychoeducation as part of patient understanding of disease. Providing information about the associated risks and the importance of treatment has shown to improve patient adherence to the treatment course [24].

Psychotherapy and medication are available options of the therapeutic plan: cognitive behavioral therapy—face to face or using online platforms—and interpersonal therapy for adolescents explore the etiology of the disorder, many studies having already confirmed their effectiveness [24]; their applicability in perinatal depression is timidly starting to be fused in current medical practice.

On the other hand, antidepressant medication is far from reaching conclusive recommendations as many clinicians are still resistant in using it since results are sometimes suspicious with some studies even suggesting a possible association with emergent suicidality [24]. The argument in relation to medication was brought into attention with the sole purpose of underlying therapeutic limitations when facing perinatal teenage depression and further intricacy of the disorder.

With restricted use of therapeutic options, complementary medicine has gained space in medical practice. There are an enormous number of products available on the market which are said to equivalate or even outreach the potential of recognized medical treatments. Only few studies actually compared the efficacy of these natural products, but what's more, evidence regarding their safety and side effects is scant. Adolescents and their parents who are reluctant to medication use sometimes opt for dietary and herbal supplements which they consider "safer," but little to no data are available on the actual effects they have on psychiatric adolescent disorders [26, 27].

In many areas around the globe, in particular in low-income countries, tradition and human connection with the environment are bound to influence medicine and the response to illness. People there consider it legitimate to refer to mother nature whenever necessary. Most interestingly, their dietary habits have come to influence clinicians around the world: having the potential to interact with other medication, physicians struggle to identify concomitant use of natural remedies when questioning patients. For instance, some authors managed to identify complementary medicine supplements most commonly used in the treatment of depression, anxiety, and attention deficit/hyperactivity disorder (ADHD). These include omega 3 fatty acids for depression and ADHD, St. John's wort, and S-adenosyl-L-methionine for depression only, while kava root, valerian root, and passionflower root were identified for generalized anxiety disorder [27, 28]. In the absence of regulatory oversight, there is a risk for all aforementioned supplements to induce serious adverse health effects.

Traditionally treated or using up-to-date medical guidelines, teenage perinatal depression is a field still waiting to be explored and conquered. The journey to recovery is usually challenging; therefore assertive parent and peer support have long shown their value in facilitating the process [24].

5. Comprehensive school reform: a possible solution?

The importance of health and sexual education in the life of teenagers has already been mentioned above, but what are the available resources we can dispose of? This matter is far more complex than it might seem at first sight. Religion, for example, has long been influencing human perception on sexuality aspects; in Ireland, Catholic "morally appropriate" sexuality education had existed for decades before the official implementation of "relationships and sexuality education" curriculum back in 1994 [29]. As Hakansson observed in his study on social judgments over abortion and contraceptive use, where there is a knowledge gap, people tend to find explanations in common beliefs in the society—these ideas being many times based on religious and cultural values [30]. This explains why current sexual education in Kenya is still focused on abstinence even though it has not been proven to reduce unintended teenage pregnancy rates [30].

In other parts of the world, accurate information on this topic is provided: the Swedish National Agency for Education has introduced biology classes in the school curriculum in which methods for preventing unwanted pregnancy are discussed starting with 7–9 school years; further in upper secondary school, topics about body changes during pregnancy are also approached [31]. With a long history of compulsory sex education starting in 1955, Swedish system has managed to adapt not only its classes to the evolving sociopolitical norms but also its teaching methods: from integration of specific subjects in generally known scientific background to individual lessons [31].

Solutions in educational system that work in one country cannot always be applied in other countries as well; differing cultural, political, and historical climates have been cited to influence this process even though scientific fundamentals of human sexual response are universal [29, 32].

There is clear evidence that proper sexuality education has a positive impact in preventing unintended adolescent pregnancies [33]. However, beside fundamental school curriculum, there are other factors to consider: the role of teachers in providing knowledge, support, and counseling as well as the involvement of physicians, parents, and outside facilitators in this process.

Although Sweden's sexuality education remains open, with no formal curriculum, teachers struggle to provide conventional information, with no specialized training taking place at the university level [29]. Society's influence on teachers often determines them to adopt stigmatizing attitudes and feel uncomfortable teaching comprehensive sexual education [30].

The absence of training is notable in medical schools as well; a worldwide survey found that up to 30% of medical schools globally have no sexual health curriculum [32]. Sexuality being a critical topic for physicians who deal with issues pertaining to reproduction and mental health, specialty education on this subject should be mandatory for aspiring clinicians [32]. To support this matter, research shows that 85% of adult patients from a US survey claimed that they would want to talk to their physician if they had a sexual problem, while 71% felt that their doctor would dismiss their concerns [34].

In the light of these disadvantageous aspects, parents are the primary source of sexuality information for their children in the United States; studies showed that transmission of information and values from parent to child can make results be more generalizable to the real world than if knowledge was taught in clinic-based sessions [35]. The Greek society, however, does not share the same beliefs: 80% of parents included in a survey considered that school is not an appropriate setting for sexual education, entrusting this task to psychologists and specialized organizations [36].

Supplementing or even replacing school lessons on sexuality, health organizations and groups often manage to implement educational initiatives to support and counsel adolescents [29].

Home education is not a tradition in Japan either; with human sexuality education introduced in 1970, school courses focus on pregnancy-related topics starting on the first year of middle school at ages 12–13 and later on the third year of middle school at ages 14–15 [36, 37].

Although health education is not the same around the world, its vital role in the future of adolescents is not to be doubted. Good understanding of sexual health promotes informed decision-making and might prevent misconceptions, fear, and unsupported cultural beliefs which are mentioned in literature as key contributors to the increase in cesarean section rates [38].

In other words, there are numerous variables which interfere with free access to education, especially health education. Along with school and any other institutions which provide knowledge on this issue, the authors, as clinicians, consider that it is also the responsibility of each physician to advise their teenage patients as well as their parents with respect to sexuality matters.

Poor acceptability of perinatal depression as a serious pathology involving life-threatening risks both on the mother and child remains a striking concern even in 2020. With 8–47% self-reported depression in perinatal teenagers [39], raising awareness among healthcare providers is legitimate. Boundaries between specialties should be seen less stringent, and as an obstetrician, monitoring of women during pregnancy and puerperium should aim to objectify both physical and mental well-being of the patient. Reaching a patient in a holistic manner can only improve the road to best medical outcomes.

6. Conclusions

Perinatal depression, although an affliction itself, should be seen as a hallmark of psychologic instability in particular when adolescent women are targeted. Dissolution of heterogeneity on the matter of access to medical care is the most powerful obstacle to overcome by physicians in the fight for health and good quality of life.

Young women having children are twice exposed to unfavorable health outcomes: first by acquiring obstetrical morbidity and mortality risks and second by having a gender-associated higher risk of developing depression during adolescence. Therefore, it is compulsory for teenage pregnant girls to become a priority on the axis of health organizations' millennial goals.

Questioning what remains to be done in this framework is an exceeding perspective in 2020; identifying and acting on key points like family authority and education environment with great impact on adolescent growth and transformation are reasonable steps to be taken in preventing teenage pregnancies. Investing in adolescents not only under economic aspects but also spiritually by providing time, receptivity, and concomitant understanding to their needs is an action that must be involved in the process.

We live in the time when artificial intelligence marked convincing results in replacing humans in various fields of activities; medicine does not make an exception, and with further comprehension that people worldwide are more connected than ever before, good practice of expert solutions has only one option: to thrive in the battle of matter over mind.

Conflict of interest

The authors declare no conflict of interest.

Author details

Alexandra Matei* and Cringu Antoniu Ionescu
Obstetrics and Gynecology Department at "St. Pantelimon" Emergency Hospital, Doctoral School "Carol Davila" University of Medicine and Pharmacy Bucharest, Bucharest, Romania

*Address all correspondence to: ale.matei@gmail.com

IntechOpen

© 2020 The Author(s). Licensee IntechOpen. This chapter is distributed under the terms of the Creative Commons Attribution License (http://creativecommons.org/licenses/by/3.0), which permits unrestricted use, distribution, and reproduction in any medium, provided the original work is properly cited.

References

[1] Adolescents overview: Investing in a safe, healthy and productive transition from childhood to adulthood is critical [Internet]. 2019. Available from: https://data.unicef.org/topic/adolescents/overview/ [Accessed: 03 March 2020]

[2] Kapungu C, Petroni S, Allen NB, et al. Gendered influences on adolescent mental health in low-income and middle-income countries: Recommendations from an expert convening. The Lancet Child & Adolescent Health. 2018;**2**(2):85-86. DOI: 10.1016/S2352-4642(17)30152-9

[3] Adolescent pregnancy [Internet]. 2020. Available from: https://www.who.int/news-room/fact-sheets/detail/adolescent-pregnancy [Accessed: 05 March 2020]

[4] Sustainable development goal 3: Ensure healthy lives and promote well-being for all at all ages: progress of goal 3 in 2019 [Internet]. Available from: https://sustainabledevelopment.un.org/sdg3 [Accessed: 26 February 2020]

[5] Mimura W, Akazawa M. The association between internet searches and moisturizer prescription in Japan: Retrospective observational study. JMIR Public Health and Surveillance. 2019;**5**(4):e13212. DOI: 10.2196/13212

[6] Eysenbach G. Infodemiology and infoveillance tracking online health information and cyberbehavior for public health. American Journal of Preventive Medicine. 2011;**40**(5 Suppl 2):S154-S158. DOI: 10.1016/j.amepre.2011.02.006

[7] Flores-Valencia ME, Nava-Chapa G, Arenas-Monreal L. Adolescent pregnancy in Mexico: A public health issue. Revista de Salud Pública (Bogotá, Colombia). 2017;**19**(3):374-378. DOI: 10.15446/rsap.v19n3.43903

[8] Holness N. A global perspective on adolescent pregnancy. International Journal of Nursing Practice. 2015;**21**(5):677-681. DOI: 10.1111/ijn.12278

[9] White L. A holistic approach to adolescent pregnancy prevention. American Journal of Public Health. 2018;**108**(Suppl 1):S4. DOI: 10.2105/AJPH.2018.304322

[10] Burrus BB. Decline in adolescent pregnancy in the United States: A success not shared by all. American Journal of Public Health. 2018;**108**(Suppl 1):S5-S6. DOI: 10.2105/AJPH.2017.304273

[11] Monteiro DLM, Martins JAFDS, Rodrigues NCP, et al. Adolescent pregnancy trends in the last decade. Revista da Associação Médica Brasileira. 2019;**65**(9):1209-1215. DOI: 10.1590/1806-9282.65.9.1209

[12] Romania has highest proportion of teenage pregnancy in EU [Internet]. 2016. Available from: https://www.neweurope.eu/article/romania-highest-proportion-teenage-pregnancy-eu/ [Accessed: 05 March 2020]

[13] Analiză privind condițiile de viață, locuire și stare de sănătate a copiilor și mamelor cu copii sub 5 ani, din mediul rural [Internet]. Available from: https://www.salvaticopiii.ro/sci-ro/files/2d/2de11e1f-1d13-469b-909d-d9eb35962229.pdf [Accessed: 26 February 2020]

[14] Semnal de alarmă: Mamele minore și copiii lor: 12.906 adolescente sub 19 ani sunt la prima naștere, 3.657 la a doua și 673 la a treia [Internet]. Available from: https://www.salvaticopiii.ro/sci-ro/files/58/58962336-d536-4fe8-a372-105bb5d96029.pdf [Accessed: 26 February 2020]

[15] Rizvi F, Williams F, Hoban E. Factors influencing unintended pregnancies amongst adolescent girls and young women in Cambodia. International Journal of Environmental Research and Public Health. 2019;**16**(20):4006. DOI: 10.3390/ijerph16204006

[16] Bas EK, Bulbul A, Uslu S, et al. Maternal characteristics and obstetric and neonatal outcomes of singleton pregnancies among adolescents. Medical Science Monitor. 2020;**26**:e919922. DOI: 10.12659/MSM.919922

[17] Wong SPW, Twynstra J, Gilliland JA, et al. Risk factors and birth outcomes associated with teenage pregnancy: A Canadian sample. Journal of Pediatric and Adolescent Gynecology. 2019;8-12. DOI: 10.1016/j.jpag.2019.10.006

[18] Sánchez Á. Embarazo en las adolescentes. Caso del Hospital Obstétrico de Pachuca, Hgo. 2005. Available from: http://dgsa.uaeh.edu.mx:8080/bibliotecadigital/handle/231104/608

[19] Dimitriu M, Ionescu CA, Matei A, et al. The problems associated with adolescent pregnancy in Romania: A cross-sectional study. Journal of Evaluation in Clinical Practice. 2019;**25**(1):117-124. DOI: 10.1111/jep.13036

[20] Teekhasaenee T, Kaewkiattikun K. Birth preparedness and complication readiness practices among pregnant adolescents in Bangkok, Thailand. Adolescent Health, Medicine and Therapeutics. 2020;**11**:1-8. DOI: 10.2147/AHMT.S236703

[21] Koo Andersson M, Tyden T. Implementation of reproductive life planning (RLP) in primary health care supported by an evidence-based website. The European Journal of Contraception & Reproductive Health Care. 2020;**25**(1):1-7. DOI: 10.1080/13625187.2019.1695117

[22] Oladeji BD, Bello T, Kola L, et al. Exploring differences between adolescents and adults with perinatal depression—Data from the expanding care for perinatal women with depression trial in Nigeria. Frontiers in Psychiatry. 2019;**10**:761. DOI: 10.3389/fpsyt.2019.00761

[23] Gureje O, Kola L, Oladeji BD, et al. Responding to the challenge of adolescent perinatal depression (RAPiD): Protocol for a cluster randomized hybrid trial of psychosocial intervention in primary maternal care. Trials. 2020;**21**:231. DOI: 10.1186/s13063-020-4086-9

[24] McIntyre R, Rong C, Subramaniapillai M, Lee Y. Major Depressive Disorder. 1st ed. St. Louis, Missouri: Elsevier; 2020. pp. 175-184

[25] Kessler RC, Avenevoli S, Ries Merikangas K. Mood disorders in children and adolescents: An epidemiologic perspective. Biological Psychiatry. 2001;**49**:1002-1014. DOI: 10.1016/S0006-3223(01)01129-5

[26] Deborah S. Complementary and integrative medicine in child and adolescent psychiatric disorders: Fact, fiction, and challenges in clinical education and residency training. Journal of the American Academy of Child and Adolescent Psychiatry. 2017;**56**(10):S116. DOI: 10.1016/j.jaac.2017.07.455

[27] Morelli V. Adolescent Health Screening: An Update in the Age of Big Data. 1st ed. St. Louis, Missouri: Elsevier; 2019. pp. 7-19

[28] Rey JM, Walter G, Soh N. Complementary and alternative medicine (CAM) treatments and pediatric psychopharmacology. Journal of the American Academy of Child and Adolescent Psychiatry. 2008;**47**(4):364-368. DOI: 10.1097/CHI.0b013e31816520e5

[29] Sherlock L. Sociopolitical influences on sexuality education in Sweden and Ireland. Sex Education. 2012;**12**(4):383-396. DOI: 10.1080/14681811.2012.686882

[30] Håkansson M, Super S, Oguttu M, et al. Social judgements on abortion and contraceptive use: A mixed methods study among secondary school teachers and student peer-counsellors in western Kenya. BMC Public Health. 2020;**20**:493. DOI: 10.1186/s12889-020-08578-9

[31] Swedish National Agency for Education. Sex Education. Gender equality, sexuality and human relationships in the Swedish Curricula: 5-13. Available from: www.skolverket.se [Accessed: 21 April 2020]

[32] Shindel AW, Baazeem A, Eardley I, et al. Sexual health in undergraduate medical education: Existing and future needs and platforms. The Journal of Sexual Medicine. 2016;**13**:1013-1026. DOI: 10.1016/j.jsxm.2016.04.069

[33] Oringanje C, Meremikwu MM, Eko H, et al. Interventions for preventing unintended pregnancies among adolescents. Cochrane Database of Systematic Reviews. 2016;**2**:CD005215

[34] Seaborne LA, Prince RJ, Kushner DM. Sexual health education in U.S. physician assistant programs. The Journal of Sexual Medicine. 2015;**12**:1158-1164. DOI: 10.1111/jsm.12879

[35] Pugliese CE, Ratto AB, Granader Y, et al. Feasibility and preliminary efficacy of a parent-mediated sexual education curriculum for youth with autism spectrum disorders. Autism. 2020;**24**(1):64-79. DOI: 10.1177/1362361319842978

[36] Hashimoto N, Shinohara H, Tashiro M, et al. Sexuality education in junior high schools in Japan. Sex Education. 2012;**12**(1):25-46. DOI: 10.1080/14681811.2011.601154

[37] Ishiwata C. Sexual health education for school children in Japan: The timing and contents. Japan Medical Association Journal. 2011;**54**(3):155-160

[38] Torloni MR, Brizuela V, Betran AP. Mass media campaigns to reduce unnecessary caesarean sections: A systematic review. BMJ Global Health. 2020;**5**:e001935. DOI: 10.1136/bmjgh-2019-001935

[39] Siegel RS, Brandon AR. Adolescents, pregnancy and mental health. Journal of Pediatric and Adolescent Gynecology. 2014;**27**:138-150. DOI: 10.1016/j.jpag.2013.09.008

Chapter 6

Working Memory, Language, Reading and Behavior: The Importance of Laterality, Symbolism and Default Networks

Levy Florence, Minshull Maryjane and Galloway-Walker Stuart

Abstract

The present review draws attention to the importance of working memory, not just for cognitive development, but also for language-related reading skills. The classical work of Patricia Goldman-Rakic drew attention to the advent of language in human development in allowing the efficient use of symbolic 'goals' to be held in working memory throughout the processes of goal achievement (sometimes over long periods of time). The role of a switching mechanism between cognitive, language and default circuits allows the recruitment of salient emotional and/or memory information during the process of goal completion. When these systems malfunction, the often-described comorbidities between conditions such as ADHD, language and learning disability, and behavior problems may be observed. At a developmental level, the capacity for symbolic representation in working memory is likely to be important for early orthographic and later comprehension in reading ability. More recent work has drawn attention to a specific role for selective cerebellar working memory selective areas such as lobules V11b/V111a in supporting parallel cortico-cerebellar visual working memory networks, a new specific role for cerebellar/cortical connections.

Keywords: working memory, language, reading, symbolic representation, brain circuits

1. Introduction

While the measurement of school readiness in preschool children has largely depended on measures of social readiness in terms of capacity to relate to peers individually and in groups, as well as capacity to follow directions, objective measures of early cognitive development are currently lacking. The present review examines early studies of Working Memory in animals and humans [1] up to current brain mapping cerebra-cortical studies [2].

Blackburne et al. [3] have drawn attention to maturational neurological differences between children and adults in recognition of typical and reversed letters. Lachman and Geyer [4] pointed out that that many of the sub-functions involved in reading are complex processes, in their own right. "For visual object recognition, symmetrically related objects are learned to be represented by similar patterns of neural activity, while such symmetry generalization is a hindrance in reading."

Levy and Young [5] demonstrated a relationship between letter reversals and attention in ADHD children. It has been shown that children especially boys who are comparatively young compared with grade peers are at risk of being labeled and treated for ADHD [6]. Additionally, such children may be disadvantaged by a maturational deficit in pre-literacy skills which continues to affect their progress in later grades. Ideally an evidence-based test of pre-literacy skills should help parents and preschool teachers in making a difficult decision currently often based on availability and cost.

Thus, according to the above authors, a failure in suppression of visually symmetrical information in the representation of visual symbols produces ambiguous relations between visual and phonological information, which can cause problems in learning to read. Duff and Clark [7] have pointed out that: "Learning to read and spell depends on grasping the principle that particular graphemes (letters) are represented by particular phonemes. Grapheme phoneme correspondence for <t> <a>, and <p> according to the authors allows application to decode 'tap', 'apt' and 'pat'.

However direct and longitudinal measurement of the relationship between orthographic and phonemic developmental skills in preschool children has not been reported. The present review draws attention to the importance of working memory, not just for cognitive development, but also for language-related reading skills. The classical work of Patricia Goldman-Rakic [1] drew attention to the advent of language in human development in allowing the efficient use of symbolic 'goals' to be held in working memory throughout the processes of goal achievement (sometimes over long periods of time). The role of a switching mechanism between cognitive, language and default circuits allow the recruitment of salient emotional and/or memory information during the process of goal completion. When these systems malfunction, the often-described comorbidities between conditions such as ADHD, language and learning disability, and behavior problems may be observed. At a developmental level the capacity for symbolic representation in working memory is likely to be important for early orthographic and later comprehension in reading ability.

2. ADHD and reading comorbidity

While comorbidity between ADHD and learning disabilities has been reported clinically for many years, few studies have investigated the frequency, and even fewer have postulated an underlying pathophysiology of this important association [8]. The authors reported that a total of 17 studies between 2001 and 2011 that examined ADHD-LD (Attention Deficit Hyperactivity-Learning Disability) comorbidity suggested a higher mean comorbidity rate (45.1%) than had been previously obtained, when reading, writing and mathematics disorders were included. The present review investigates the key role of language and reading abilities in human working memory and relation to ADHD and learning disability. The development of linguistic representation has allowed increased capacity for task achievement and planning, as well as working memory integration of verbal and visual symbolism important for reading and spelling. Cognitive mechanisms that facilitate appropriate switching between executive and default networks is also discussed in relation to possible comorbid ADHD-LD deficits.

Tierney and Nelson [9] have discussed brain development and the role of experience in the early years. The authors described the importance early synaptogenesis and subsequent synaptic pruning [10] in the laying down of language and facial processing systems as the basis for later cognitive and emotional functions. An important modulator of early behavior is the capacity for maintenance of a goal in working memory. While primates are characterized by advanced development of binocular vision resulting in stereoscopic depth perception, specialization of the hands and feet for grasping, and enlargement of the cerebral hemispheres, humans are importantly capable of symbolic working memory goals.

3. Representation of discriminative stimuli

Goldman-Rakic [1, 11, 12] described the importance of activity in the prefrontal cortex during working memory tasks and the ability to guide behavior by representations of discriminative stimuli rather than by the discriminative stimuli themselves as a "major achievement of evolution." According to Goldman-Rakic [1], this capacity was shown to depend on the bilateral integrity of the dorsolateral prefrontal cortex [13, 14]. The, capacity was believed to have mnemonic, temporal-sequential, spatial perception/orientation and attentional and motor control functions that allowed correct responses and disallowed or inhibited incorrect responses. Goldman-Rakic [11] drew attention to the distinction between working and associative memory, and the pre-eminent role of the prefrontal cortex in the former. She found that the dorsolateral prefrontal cortex (PFC) contained a local circuit that encompassed short-term memory, attentional and response control mechanisms in the principal sulcus of the dorsolateral PFC (DLPFC) and postulated a superior to inferior localization of spatial, object and linguistic processing with a common architecture for their network organization. She also described parallel connections with the posterior parietal cortex and feature working memory areas of the inferior prefrontal cortex and area TE in the temporal lobe. Posterior parietal regions were believed to carry **directionally specific** information in all phases of the delayed response task from cue to delay and response and to mirror those in the prefrontal cortex. She proposed that the central executive should be considered as an "emergent property of co-activation of multiple parallel domain-specific processors located in the PFC and interconnected with domain-relevant long-term storage sites in the posterior sensory regions of the cortex and appropriate motor pathways" [11]. Levy and Farrow [15] discussed the role of prefrontal/parietal connections in sustaining activation during an A-X continuous performance task and facilitation by administration of methylphenidate. The classical work of Goldman-Rakic in drawing attention to the central role of **representational** cuing ability in working memory is central to the present argument.

4. Current brain mapping

If we fast-forward to current bran-mapping approaches to large-scale brain systems, Castellanos and Proal [16] have postulated a number of "resting state" and candidate neural and attentional systems, thought to be of importance in ADHD psychopathology. Interestingly they describe a "dorsal attentional network, which mediated goal-directed, top-down executive control processes, particularly in re-orienting attention during visual attentional functioning, with key nodes in the intraparietal sulcus (BA40) and the frontal eye fields ((BA6), the latter being perhaps the converse mirror image of the DLPFC above".

The work of Sonuga-Barke and Castellanos [17] drew attention to the "anti-correlation" of executive vs. default networks for ADHD, suggesting that ADHD was characterized by inappropriate default intrusions during working memory. Mechanisms that control the rapid and transient switches from executive to default mode are not well understood. Menon and Uddin [18] have postulated that the anterior insula and the anterior cingulate cortex form a "salience network," "that functions to segregate the most relevant among internal and extra-personal stimuli in order to guide behavior." The authors described two critical networks whose activation and deactivation is observed during cognitive tasks: the central executive network and the default network. The former was thought to include the dorsolateral prefrontal cortex (DLPFC), posterior parietal cortex (PFC), while the default mode network included the ventromedial prefrontal cortex (VMPFC) and posterior cingulate cortex. While the central executive was important for the active maintenance and manipulation of working memory during goal-directed behavior, the default network including medial temporal lobe and angular gyrus, in addition to PCC and VMPFC, were active during tasks that involved autobiographical memory and self-reference. Furthermore, a third coupling of the anterior insula (AI) and anterior cingulate cortex (ACC) was thought to be "involved in transient detection of salient stimuli and initiating attentional control signals, which are then sustained by the ACC and the ventrolateral and dorsolateral PFC."

The AI was believed by Menon and Uddin [18] to have a critical role in switching between large-scale networks to facilitate the saliency of attention and working memory resources. Importantly, the AI and ACC have been found to contain von Economo neurons (VEN's) with large axons that facilitated rapid relay of AI and ACC signals to other cortical regions, and function as a switch mechanism between central executive and default mode. The authors postulate that AI pathology could account for deficits in social processing in conditions such as autism when hypoactive, as well as auditory verbal hallucinations when hyperactive, and attentional deficits in a number of pathological conditions.

Allman et al. [19] described the presence of VEN's in humans and apes only. The authors utilized diffusion tensor imaging in a gorilla brain to show connection of VEN-containing regions to frontal and insular cortex, septum and amygdala. They postulated that VEN's activity could be evolutionarily derived from gut/appetite monitoring at neuronal level, allowing rapid reactions to changing conditions. (Wikipedia suggests that significant olfactory and gustatory capabilities of the ACC and fronto-insular cortex have been usurped during recent evolution to serve enhanced roles in higher cognition). Fajardo et al. [20] also described a group of cells with similar morphology to VENS in the dorsolateral prefrontal cortex of humans (described by Goldman-Rakic [1] as important for working memory functions).

5. Default language network, reading and development

The importance of working memory for reading comprehension was studied by Gonzalez-Perez et al. [21] who investigated electrophysiological correlates in 52 Spanish ADHD children divided into those with and without reading comprehension deficits. The authors pointed out that "working memory is essential for reading sentences because noun and verb phrases tend to be situated apart from each other, and they need to be maintained and attached in the proper order to be comprehended." For anaphoretic phrases (the use of a word, referring back to a word used earlier in a text or conversation, to avoid repetition, e.g., pronouns), the gender of a subject and its pronouns are the only clues to achieve agreement. Where there is gender or number disagreement, electrophysiological evoked potential (ERP) recordings of components such as early left anterior negativity (ELAN) and left anterior negativity (LAN) and P 600 are affected. ELA is described as emerging 200 ms after stimulus presentation, whereas LAN is seen at from 350 to 550 ms, and believed to represent the first syntactic parsing of sentences using lexical information. On the other hand, P600 is a later component, seen between 500 and 900 ms, also reflecting agreement violations and possible attempts to repair incorrect alignments. Gonzalez-Perez et al. [21] utilized ERP measurements in ADHD children with and without reading comprehension deficits and normal controls. They demonstrated that ADHD children without reading comprehension deficits and control children began morphosyntactic agreement processing in the first 100 ms after the appearance of a target, while the ADHD children with reading comprehension difficulty appeared to begin this processing 250 ms after appearance of the target, suggesting impairment of working memory processes in reading comprehension in those children.

6. Linguistic approaches to working memory

In relation to symbolic aspects of working memory, it is useful to compare Spanish, French and English linguistic (anaphoretic) experiments; in that, Spanish and French languages utilize gender-based pronouns for both people and objects, while in similar English experiments, gender is specifically related to people. Carreiras et al. [22] investigated 'surface' pronouns in three Spanish language experiments in which non-semantic gender pronouns matched their antecedents on the basis of 'morphosyntactic' properties alone. That interpretation of pronouns referring to things was speeded by a syntactic gender match. Garnham et al. [23] reported three similar experiments in Spanish and French in which the interpretation and response times of pronouns for morphological vs. semantic (superficial vs. deep) anaphors. By including results from sentences about people and sentences about things, the investigators demonstrated that reading times for subordinate clauses were read more quickly when there was a gender cue. This effect was equally large for people and things, but stronger for people references when subsequently questioned. In a third French experiment the authors found that while the gender cue in pronouns about things was strong, this 'superficial' representation became less readily available over time, when grammatical or semantic references became more important.

Friedman et al. [24] have investigated ADHD and working memory's contribution to reading comprehension and applied maths problem-solving abilities. The authors describe working memory (WM) as a "limited capacity, multi-component system responsible for temporarily storing and processing sensory information." They suggest that the working component of WM or Central Executive (CE) is "responsible for focusing attention, inhibiting irrelevant information from accessing focused attention, and updating, manipulating and reordering information stored within two anatomically distinct subsidiary memory systems-the phonological (PH) and visuospatial (VS) short-term memory subsystems-which are responsible for the temporary storage and maintenance of verbal and non-verbal visual/spatial information, respectively." According to the above authors, few studies have examined the hypothesis that WM plays key roles in reading comprehension (and applied mathematics). These studies have found that phonological WM (using CE and PS STM and/or visuospatial VS STM) jointly contributed to reading comprehension. However, they found that no study had dissociated the three important WM components (CE, PHSTM and VSSTM) to determine their unique contributions to the difficulties of children with ADHD.

Friedman et al. [24] compared two groups of children aged 8–12 years, namely a group with ADHD Combined Inattention/Hyperactivity and a typically developing group. They utilized computerized - phonological and visuospatial working memory tasks. According to the authors, these tasks measure the ability to mentally store, rehearse and manipulate the serial order of verbal or spatial stimuli. Additionally, reading comprehension (KTEA Reading Comprehension standardized four potential mediating variables: subtest scores as well as Orthographic Conversion scores were analyzed. The latter factor score reflected an estimate of overall orthographic conversion ability via an Orthographic Conversion Speed Task and a KTEA Reading Recoding/Letter-Word task [24]. The investigators analyzed four potential mediating variables, PHSTM, VSSTM, CE and Orthographic conversion to determine whether they independently contributed to ADHD-related Reading Comprehension difficulties. Only CE and Orthographic Conversion were found to emerge as significant partial indicators of the relation between Diagnostic Status and Reading Comprehension. Subsequent modeling indicated that the collective influence of CE and Orthographic Conversion fully accounted for between-group differences in reading comprehension and explained 61% of the variance between diagnostic status and reading comprehension. The authors commented that the failure of some computer-based WM interventions could be explained by misspecification of intervention targets. The study highlights the association of central executive working memory and visuospatial orthographic processes affecting reading in ADHD children. The latter effect may indicate a representational cuing effect, as originally described by Goldman-Rakic [1].

7. Maturation effects

Friederici, Brauer and Lohman [25] have described a maturational functional re-organization of the neural network, underlying language development, believed to allow a close interplay between frontal and temporal regions within the left hemisphere. The investigators utilized correlational methods, based on the analysis of low frequency fluctuations, previously used in resting state studies. They were able to identify a network with a strong correlation between the ventral part of the inferior frontal gyrus (IFG) and superior temporal sulcus (STS)/superior temporal gyrus (STG/STS).

The above authors investigated age-related comparisons of six-year old children and adults that demonstrated important differences between the child and adult subjects, using an auditory sentence comprehension paradigm. They analyzed functional connectivity between the left inferior frontal cortex and the posterior superior temporal gyrus (STG/STS). Their statistical analyses concentrated on perisylvan areas in the inferior frontal and superior temporal cortices in both hemispheres. "When seeded in the left, Brocas Area 44 (BA44), strong correlations were obtained with the left posterior temporal cortex in adults, whereas in children no such ipsilateral correlation was observed," but "children showed stronger correlations of BA44 with the contralateral inferior frontal region." The authors suggested that a general lateralization principle underlying the normal development of cognitive processes applied to the development of the default network for language.

Tomasi and Volkow [26] investigated the maturation, during childhood and adolescence, of functional connectivity of the substantia nigra vs. ventral tegmental areas in 402 healthy children/adolescents and 704 healthy young adults, as well as 203 children with ADHD. The investigators pointed out that VTA midbrain neurons give rise to the mesocorticolimbic pathway, while the substantia nigra midbrain DA neurons give rise to the nigrostriatal pathway. The investigators mapped functional connectivity orthogonal resting state patterns, utilizing brief magnetic resonance imaging (MRI). They demonstrated reproducible VTA and SN connectivity patterns. Interestingly, typically developing children (TDC) showed preferential VTA connection with subthalamic nucleus, globus pallidus, thalamus and vermis, while for adults VTA was additionally connected with the mesolimbic pathway (nucleus accumbens, hippocampus and para-hippocampus) and with the anterior insula. Thus, according to the authors, limbic regions showed strong connection with VTA in adults, but an unexpected strong connection with SN in typically developing children. There were also strong lateralization effects in Broca's (cortical area involved with speech production and Wernicke's cortical area involved in speech reception) that were more pronounced in adults. The investigators interpreted their results as showing age-related increases in functional connectivity of the VTA with limbic regions and the default mode network, and by decreases in connectivity of the SN with motor and medial temporal cortices, indicating a change from SN influences in childhood/young adolescence and a combined SN and VTA influence in young adulthood. Furthermore ROI (region of interest) analysis showed that ADHD children had stronger SN connectivity in left amygdala and insula than normally developing children, and stronger VTA connectivity in thalamus, subthalamic nucleus and globus pallidus than TDC. This pattern was thought to be consistent with delayed maturational pruning of the connectivity patterns in these regions.

8. Discussion

A number of differing research approaches and the advent of sophisticated brain mapping techniques have drawn attention to the importance of default mode access and regulation in both normal and pathological working memory regulation processes. Executive function is thought to depend on cortico-striatal-thalamic-cortical integrity [27], while the default mode is postulated as an associative, internally directed and 'anti-correlated' network, with overlapping hubs related to semantics, salience and language [28]. It is now believed that far from a passive resting cognition, default cognitions have important integrative roles in both utilizing past salient memories and establishing future orientations. Importantly, the control of ongoing switching activity between executive and default circuits may be central in determining when and whether default activities, such as day-dreaming and fantasy are productive or pathological. In the present context, the linguistic use of pronoun gender anaphors are an example of representational cues used to maintain comprehension of separated noun/verb clauses. In this respect, von Economo cells in the anterior insula have appeared to be one central area in switching rapidly from default, language and salience circuits to executive functions. Executive functions are feedback controlled and relate back to representations in the prefrontal cortex, while the default mode associations are thought to help integrate emotionally based experiences and recollections of episodic memory. Optimal cognitive function requires smooth transition between executive (external) and internal (default) cognitions. When these switching mechanisms are impaired, pathological conditions such as ADHD, autism and behavior disorder may develop.

The present review draws attention to the importance of working memory, not just for cognitive development, but also for language-related reading skills. In this regard, the advent of language in human development has allowed the efficient use of symbolic 'goals' to be held in working memory throughout the processes of goal achievement (sometimes over long periods of time). In addition, the description of a switching mechanism between cognitive, language and default circuits facilitate the recruitment of salient emotional and/or memory information during the process of goal completion. When these systems malfunction, the often-described comorbidities between conditions such as ADHD, language and learning disability, behavior problems (and autistic syndromes) may be observed. At a developmental level the capacity for symbolic representation in working memory is likely to be important both for early orthographic and later comprehension in reading ability.

The interaction of language, early reading and attentional skills has important implications for future studies of kindergarten readiness and gender differences in preschool children. Additionally, a recent review of cerebellar effects on fast-acting internal brain models, has described both forward and reverse effects on both tool use and cognitive functions [29]. Forward models are able to update internal circuits with rapid effects on cortical and subcortical structures, allowing adaption of motor performance errors. However, addition, there are hypotheses that the cerebellum is involved in modification of language processing, particularly in correction of well-established semantic processes. The addition of rapid cerebellar corrections with maturity, adds an error correction component to cortical, subcortical and cerebellar circuits involved in language development.

Author details

Levy Florence[1*], Minshull Maryjane[2] and Galloway-Walker Stuart[3]

1 Child and Family East, Prince of Wales Hospital and University of New South Wales, Sydney, NSW, Australia

2 KU Peter Pan La Perouse Preschool, Sydney, Australia

3 ICT Consultant, JGW Consulting, Hobart, Tasmania, Australia

*Address all correspondence to: f.levy@unsw.edu.au

IntechOpen

© 2019 The Author(s). Licensee IntechOpen. This chapter is distributed under the terms of the Creative Commons Attribution License (http://creativecommons.org/licenses/by/3.0), which permits unrestricted use, distribution, and reproduction in any medium, provided the original work is properly cited.

References

[1] Goldman-Rakic P. Development of cortical circuitry and cognitive function. Child Development. 1987;**58**(3):601-622

[2] Brissenden JA, Tobyne SM, Osher DE, Levin EJ, Halko MA, Somers DC. Topographic cortico-cerebellar networks revealed by visual attention and working memory. Current Biology. 2018;**28**(21):3364-3372 e5

[3] Blackburne LK, Eddy MD, Kalra P, Yee D Sinha P, et al. Neural correlates of letter reversal in children and adults. PLoS One. 2014;**9**(5):e98386

[4] Lachman T, Geyer T. Letter reversals in dyslexia: Is the case really closed? A critical review and conclusions. Psychology Science. 2003;**45**:50-72

[5] Levy F, Young D. Letter reversals, default mode, and childhood ADHD. Journal of Attention Disorders. 2016. DOI: 10.1177/1087054715624229

[6] Layton TJ, Barnett ML, Hicks TR, Jena AB. Attention-deficit-hyperactivity disorder and month of school enrolment. New England Journal of Medicine. 2018;**379**:2122-2130

[7] Duff FJ, Clarke PJ. Practitioner review: Reading disorders—What are effective interventions and how should they be implemented and evaluated? Journal of Child Psychology & Psychiatry. 2011;**52**:3-12

[8] DuPaul GJ, Gormley MJ, Laracy SD. Comorbidity of LD and ADHD: Implications of DSM-5 for assessment and treatment. Journal of Learning Disabilities. 2012:1-6. DOI: 10.1177/0022219412464351

[9] Tierney AL, Nelson CA. Brain development and the role of experience in the early years. Zero Three. 2009;**30**(2):9-13

[10] Huttenlocher PR, Dabholkar AS. Regional differences in synaptogenesis in human cerebral cortex. The Journal of Comparative Neurology. 1997;**387**:167-178

[11] Goldman-Rakic PS, Cools AR, Srivastava K. The prefrontal landscape: Implications of functional architecture for understanding human mentation and the central executive. Philosophical Transactions: Biological Sciences. 1996;**351**(1346):1445-1453

[12] Rosvold HE, Mirsky AF, Sarason I, Bransome ED, Beck LH. A continuous performance test of brain damage. Journal of Consulting Psychology. 1956;**20**(5):343-350

[13] Goldman-Rakic PS. Architecture of the prefrontal cortex and the central executive. Annals of the New York Academy of Sciences. 1995;**15**(769):71-83

[14] Goldman-Rakic PS. Topography of cognition: Parallel distributed networks in primate association cortex. Annual Review of Neuroscience. 1988;**11**:137-156. DOI: 10.1146/annurev.ne.11.030188.001033

[15] Levy F, Farrow M. Working memory in ADHD: Prefrontal/parietal connections. Current Drug Targets. 2001;**2**:347-352

[16] Castellanos FX, Proal E. Large-scale brain systems in ADHD: Beyond the prefrontal-striatal model. Trends in Cognitive Science. 2012;**16**(1):17-26

[17] Sonuga-Barke EJ, Castellanos. Spontaneous attentional fluctuations in impaired states and pathological conditions: A neurobiological hypothesis. Neuroscience & Biobehavioral Reviews. 2007;**31**:977-986

[18] Menon V, Uddin LQ. Saliency, switching, attention and control: A

network model of insula function. Brain Structure and Function. 2010;**214**(5-6):655-667

[19] Allman JM, Tetrealt NA, Hakeem AT, Allman JM, Teatrealt NA, Hakeem AY, et al. The von Economo neurons in frontoinsular and anterior cingulate cortex in great apes and humans. Brain Structure and Function. 2010;**214**(5-6):495-517

[20] Fajardo C, Escobar MI, Buritica E, Artega G, Umbarilla J, Casanova MF, et al. Von Economo neurons are present in the dorsolateral (dysgranular) prefrontal cortex of humans. Neuroscience Letters. 2008;**435**:215-218

[21] Gonzalez-Perez PA, Hernandez-Exposito S, Perez J, Ramirez G, Dominguez A. Electrophysiological correlates of reading in children with attention deficit hyperactivity disorder. Revista de Neurologia. 2018;**66**(6):175-181

[22] Carreiras M, Garnham A, Oakhill JV. The use of superficial and meaning-based representations in interpreting pronouns: Evidence from Spanish. European Journal of Cognitive Psychology. 1993;**5**:93-116

[23] Garnham A, Oakhill J, Erlich M-F. Representations and processes in the interpretation of pronouns: New evidence from Spanish and French. Journal of Memory and Language. 1995;**34**:41-62

[24] Friedman LM, Rapport MD, Calub CA, Eckrich SJ. ADHD and core foundational learning: Working Memory's contribution to reading to reading comprehension and Applied Math problem-solving abilities. The ADHD Report. 2018;**26**(7):1-7

[25] Friederici AD, Brauer J, Lohman G. Maturation of the language network: From inter- to intra-hemispheric connectivities. PLoS One. 2011;**6**(6):e20726

[26] Tomasi D, Volkow N. Abnormal functional connectivity in children with attention-deficit/hyperactivity disorder. Biological Psychiatry. 2012;**71**(5):443-450

[27] Levy F, Young D. Letter reversals, default mode, and childhood ADHD. Journal of Attention Disorders. 2014. DOI: 10.1177/1087054715624229

[28] Balleine BW, O'Doherty JP. Human and rodent homologies in action control: Corticostriatal determinants of goal-directed and habitual action. Neuropsychopharmacology. 2010;**35**(1):48-69

[29] Popa LS, Ebner TJ. Cerebellum and Internal Models. In: Manto M, Gruol D, Schmahmann J, Koibuchi N, Sillitoe R, editors. Handbook of the Cerebellum and Cerebellar Disorders. Springer; 2019. DOI: 10.1007/978-3-319-97911-3_56-2

Lightning Source UK Ltd.
Milton Keynes UK
UKHW051947140222
398697UK00005B/576